Family Matters

*Lessons on Living, Dying &
Leaving Our Stuff Behind*

ANN MARQUEZ

Desert Muse Publishing

Desert Muse Publishing, desertmuse19@gmail.com
All rights reserved.

Ann Marquez/Desert Muse Publishing
Fairacres, NM

ISBN-13:
    978-0-9815336-1-2 (paperback)
    978-0-9815336-2-9 (epub)
    978-0-9815336-3-6 (mobi)

Library of Congress Control Number: 2018913751

Family Matters is a collection of personal essays and case studies. With the exception of contributions made by my sister Connie, and my daughter Shelley, the stories shared, information gathered, and conclusions drawn are based solely upon my perspective as a daughter and personal representative to a dysfunctional estate. Readers are responsible for consulting their own legal, financial and medical professionals before implementing any plan of action.

Scripture taken from the *Holy Bible, New International Version®*. Copyright © 1973,1978, 1984 by International Bible Society. Used by permission of Zondervan Publishing House. All rights reserved.

The "NIV" and "New International Version" trademarks are registered in the United States Patent and Trademark Office by International Bible Society. Use of either trademark requires the permission of International Bible Society.

Grateful acknowledgments are made to:

The Liberace Foundation for permission to reprint excerpts from *The Things I Love* by Wladzin Valentino Liberace. © The Liberace Foundation for the Performing and Creative Arts 1976. *The mission of the Liberace Foundation is to help talented students pursue careers in the performing and creative arts through scholarship assistance.* Liberace.org

Roy E. Perry for permission to print poems "Dawn and Dusk" and "Precious and Princess." © Roy E. Perry.

Family Matters/ Ann Marquez. – 1st ed.

*To those who have passed on
before us*

*For those we must someday
leave behind*

Contents

Author's Note: v
About This Edition vii
Prologue xi
There Are No Guarantees in Estate Planning 1
Waking Dreams 7
In the In-between 17
Flight 31
Going Home: A Place of Rest 35
Direction 45
Kindred 49
In the Beginning, Dreadful Confusion That Was 55
The Safe Deposit Box 71
Send in the Clowns 77
Self-worth 83
Will Your Estate Be a Financial Burden? 93
I'll Be Dissin' You, Always 105
A Hug from Mabel 111
Ransacked 117
Grave Decisions 127
Soul Searching 135
What's That Rattling? 143
Guessing Game 147
A Winter Festival 155
In the Ending That Finally Was Found 167
About the Author 173

Author's Note:

After two-years' worth of publishing delays, it took a pandemic—Covid-19—to finally get this edition into print and "into the world."

Like many of you, the Great Pause gave me space and time to reevaluate priorities and to sort through and untangle life's necessities from the superfluous. When our state's stay-at-home orders went into effect, my husband was stuck working out of town, and I spent those first five weeks home alone. Unlike our toilet paper supply, I had time and space aplenty.

I think it was somewhere around week number four when my walls began closing in along with the boxes and tubs and files and flash drives strewn throughout my house, that overflowed with mostly incomplete, unpublished work. Haunting me and taunting me, surrounded by so much unfinished business, I revisited a few of the existential questions posed in *Family Matters*—

If I died today, would my life be released into peace? Or entangled by regret? Will it matter that I was?

Ironically, earlier that month, as another scheduled publishing date approached, I had felt it would be wrong to release and promote this book during a time when so many people were dying. I couldn't fathom taking advantage of such a horrific, ongoing tragedy.

Still, the death count in New York continued to rise. Heart wrenching stories of lives cut short, people who were *here* and then *gone,* just like that, consumed my TV viewing time. A constant, overwhelming sense of fragility and uncertainty took hold. Urgency replaced my reluctance and publishing this book became a matter of if not now, when?

This is my now.

Thank you for choosing *Family Matters*. Stay safe out there. Wash your hands. Wear your mask. Be kind to one another. ♡

About This Edition

Early one morning my friend, Janet, called to say, "I just read your book!"

I was confused. Having recently sent her a 4-H cookbook as a gift, I asked, "You read the cookbook?"

"NO!" she laughed. "I just read *your* book, and I owe you an apology."

An apology? Three full years had passed since I mailed Janet a newly published copy of *Journey into Probate and Back*. What in the world could she be talking about?

"When I received your book, I looked at the cover and thought, *I don't want to read a stuffy old book about probate*. So, I stashed it on a shelf until last night.

It isn't stuffy at all! Why didn't you tell me it has these wonderful stories inside?"

A couple of years later, another friend gave a copy to an acquaintance, a clairvoyant named Laurie, who was battling a terminal illness. One day Laurie called, introduced herself, thanked me for sharing my experiences, and declared: "We must find a way to get these delicious stories out into the world!"

I got a kick out of how she called my stories delicious.

Weeks later, when she called a second time to encourage me to find a way to market the book, I shared my ideas about publishing an updated version: with a new title, a new cover, a new start. She gave me one of those long, awkward, soul-searching pauses, and then simply responded, "No."

I didn't ask why.

Sadly, Laurie passed away shortly afterward. And each time I thought about that last conversation, I've felt that it would probably be a bad idea to go against her advice. Besides, having spent years writing three versions of *Journey into Probate and Back*, publishing, and then letting it go out of print, I really haven't been interested in spending too much time on changes, additions, or updates. My heart just isn't in it for many reasons. I've moved on to other topics.

On the other hand, Laurie had been clear that my book was personally meaningful. The memory of her enthusiasm nagged at me so much over the years that I've finally decided to give in and release the stories into the world. But this decision didn't come easy.

You see, over a decade ago, my first journey into self-publishing created its own story, ripe with unexpected obstacles, plenty of potholes, a sinkhole or two—and a learning curve. To me, the original title perfectly represented my experience, from finding out about my father's estate and having to go down the rabbit hole of lawyers and probate ("In the Beginning, Dreadful Confusion That Was") to a Dante-inspired ending ("It was from there that we emerged, to see—once more—the stars").

I never expected that the word probate would be a barrier. To this day, people see that title and say, "I don't need to know about probate"; or "I don't have anything to leave behind"; or "I don't have an estate (chuckle)." One woman looked over my book and said, "All I have to leave behind is my cat. My neighbor in the apartment next door will take her if anything happens to me."

I wanted to ask, "Will she? Really? How can you be so sure?"

To my further surprise, I also learned that a lot of people don't even know what probate is. More than one person has told me they had to look up the word. Some thought it had to do with probation and gave me a suspicious glance.

Early on, after explaining the concept to a potential editor, the gruff old man shot back, "No one is going to want to read a book about a daughter complaining about her father."

After I published, the man became one of my biggest fans. "How are sales?" he asked one day in passing.

"No sales," I replied.

"That's too bad. It's a good book."

Encouraged by such memories, and with lessons learned, *Family Matters* comes free of my former ambition, believing that I could encourage families to mend broken relationships and address end-of-life issues—before it's too late. I've realized that was a lofty goal.

Now, my simple wish is that you find this edition interesting at least, and helpful at best. Most of all, I hope you'll find at least a couple of my stories—delicious.

Prologue

In 2007, I attended a community-sponsored estate planning seminar presented by an attorney from a local law firm. Rows of chairs filled the spacious conference room in anticipation of a crowd. I was the first to arrive and, as it turned out, the only official attendee. (According to the attorney, although the three other ladies in attendance had voiced genuine interest in the subject, each did not count because they were library employees connected to the event.)

The attorney paced in front of the lectern while waiting for late-comers and reminisced aloud about a time "up until about five years ago" when an estate and trust seminar would pack the room. After conceding defeat, he began his talk with a condensed explanation of what an estate is. Next he gave the standard rendition of why probate is bad and why a living trust arrangement is good. Last he explained how a trust is created, and he concluded with assurance that when the creator of a trust dies, his trustee distributes his property without problem: Happy Ending.

From the first seminar I had attended years before, to this one, and to all in-between, nothing had changed. The original promise and hype over the living trust had brought us back to the same old tired quandary:

"What would prevent the trustee from abusing the trust?" I asked.

With an appearance of caught-off-guard-reluctance, the attorney admitted, "Nothing."

To my surprise he shared a tale about a grandmother who had been in charge of her grandchild's inheritance. Instead of protecting and preserving the assets for the child, she cashed in and went on a shopping spree. By the time his firm discovered her offense, it was too late. The grandmother had blown tens of thousands of dollars and her grandchild was out of luck.

When the firm confronted the grandmother about her—shall we say, mismanagement—she exclaimed, "But our family had a wonderful Christmas!"

I asked what happened to the grandmother. Again, the answer was nothing. The attorney said he did attempt to bring the infraction before a judge—*seeing how her actions were technically embezzlement*—but the judge simply asked, "What do you want me to do? Throw a grandmother in jail?"

So, there we have it. There are no magical arrangements. A living trust faces the same exposure to abuse as the probate estate. And as long as we continue to trek along the same path of fearing probate and taxes, of creating estate plans in secret, of hiding assets and information, of leaving this world with unresolved relationships, and of focusing on protecting our assets over our heirs, the problems and abuse will remain.

The following stories are intended neither as legal or financial advice, nor as a substitute for such advice. After decades of attorney-authored estate planning books centered on saving taxes, avoiding probate, and controlling heirs, *Journey into Probate and Back*, and its new edition *Family Matters*, provides a long-neglected view from the other side—the human side.

I walk alone down a long, barren hallway illuminated by a soft overhead glow. Another hallway cuts across my path and stretches into obscurity. A door appears at the corner where the hallways merge. I try to open it, but it is locked. The wall above begins to crack and peel away, allowing a small shaft of light to pierce through. I want to look inside, but the opening is beyond my reach.

To my right appears a second door, framed in radiant light; this one opens. The room is empty except for one folding chair in the center. Six doors line the back wall. I try to run toward the one on the far right, but something blocks my path. Desperate to leave, I try for another on the left, but I can't move. There is no escape other than to awaken.

Each time I'm drawn into this recurring nightmare, a larger area of wall breaks away until—at last—I am able to raise myself up and peer inside. The room is in total chaos with all sorts of papers tossed about everywhere. I recognize the desk, the chair, the filing cabinet.

It is my father's room.

JOURNAL ENTRY, MAY 1988

Death always creates unfinished business.

I hated all the things I had toiled for under the sun, because I must leave them to the one who comes after me. And who knows whether he will be a wise man or a fool? Yet he will have control over all the work into which I have poured my effort and skill under the sun. This too is meaningless.

So my heart began to despair over all my toilsome labor under the sun. For a man may do his work with wisdom, knowledge, and skill, and then he must leave all he owns to someone who has not worked for it. This too is meaningless and a great misfortune.

What does a man get for all the toil and anxious striving with which he labors under the sun? All his days his work is pain and grief; even at night his mind does not rest. This too is meaningless.

ECCLESIASTES 2:18-23
AUTHOR BELIEVED TO BE KING SOLOMON

There Are No Guarantees in Estate Planning

Despite what an attorney or financial advisor might advise, despite creating a clear, legal, safeguarded will, and despite the best of intentions—you do not have absolute control over your final instructions, your choice of representative, or your choice of heir(s). Even a valid directive over your own body can be easily overlooked or disregarded by the unwilling and the unforeseen.

Perhaps the greatest estate planning misconception of all is that your attorney and the court are obligated to enforce your instructions once you are gone.

Maybe they will. Maybe they won't.

You may have written specific instructions in your will document, but just because you said so does not mean that these instructions are valid in your state, or that your executor will follow them. You may "nominate" a guardian for your minor child, but a court will have the final say. And if you have assumed there exists some sort of estate/probate police, ready and set to protect your assets, guess what? No one is going to physically patrol your estate or keep a vigilant eye on *all* your worldly possessions to see that every single thing is properly distributed.

When the situation goes wrong and things go missing, don't count on anyone in the legal world to give a hoot as to how you really intended for things to go. And if your personal relationships were a mess, the truth is an attorney isn't going to get down and dirty in the family mud, unless your estate's bottom line is well worth his time (as one lawyer confided in me).

More than two thousand years after The Book of Ecclesiastes was recorded (c. 450-200 BCE), despite untold legal, social, and technological advances, we remain as bound to the same rule of uncertainty as old King Solomon: Who will be our heirs, and how will they behave?

Days of Yore—Grandmother lived a simple, predictable life. She always commuted by bus, never applied for a credit card, always stayed on budget, saved for whatever she bought, and simply did without for what she couldn't afford. Going shopping was an event, not a whim. When she died, her assets included a modest checking and savings account at the local bank, one mortgage-free house, a modest life insurance policy, and proudly grown stock in Nucor Steel.

Spanning the decades in her serene Kansas home, Grandmother owned one telephone, one "ice box," one black-and-white television set, and the same eclectic mix of furnishings. There was never any thought of remodeling, redecorating, or refinancing. Possessions were few—but meaningful—and never, ever, taken for granted.

After her funeral, Dad spoke with inspired appreciation of how convenient she had made things for him. From prepaid funeral arrangements to the effortless transfer of property into his name, Grandmother had prepared a thoughtful estate.

"She expects me to do the same for my children," Dad reflected with pride. But on that day, he could not see the next twenty years' worth of life events—and a lot can change in twenty years.

Today's estate can include so much more. There may be CDs, 401(k)s, annuities, IRAs, pensions, several life insurance policies, Health Savings Account (HSA) or Medicare Advantage (MSA) benefits, stock portfolios, personal stock, investment property, lawsuit settlements or outstanding personal loans to collect, precious metal investments, time shares, limited partnerships, royalties, copyrights, patents, frequent-flyer miles, reward points, pin numbers, eBay and Amazon accounts, social media accounts, cyber currency, collectibles, storage units, and a safe deposit box or two.

More Americans are living in stepfamily settings rather than traditional nuclear family households. People are living longer and remarrying late in life, creating stepfamily situations devoid of deep personal attachments. When these estates combine, family heirlooms, family histories—entire inheritances—risk becoming lost to the control of strangers.

An estate may be tangled in an enormous amount of debt. There may be a pending bankruptcy, accelerated death benefits from a life insurance policy, viatical settlement, or a reverse mortgage to consider.

Email accounts, passwords, cell phone access, and hard drives have become sources of contention between obligation and implied privacy. During the time of my father's probate, mega-mergers and outsourcing by financial institutions created mindless, impersonal staff, which affected efficiency, accountability, and the security of account information being transferred from hard copy to data entries.

Matters of organ donation, harvesting, stem cells, frozen sperm, frozen eggs, and DNA are all vulnerable to outside intrusion.

In 2005, the world sat ringside to the drama of Terri Schiavo, while her very soul was held hostage in legal battle limbo between the human ability to prolong life and life's inevitable release. No longer a matter of nature, personal or sacred, any and all life might now be used as a political pawn by Congress, as twenty-four-hour news fodder for the outrage/hate-mongering talk-show cause of the month, or the religious cause of the month because, ironically, many hold a tremendous fear of granting God full control over death—of trusting the soul to "go home to God."

Doctors, caretakers, or pharmacists may attempt to control matters of life, death, or the needs of others based upon their own ethics or political standards, overriding the personal instruction of patient or family. Medical treatments might be forced upon or denied to an individual, depending upon one's financial situation or available health insurance coverage.

Estate issues have become far too complex to be entrusted to a simple will created by a detached attorney or a homemade will kit. Naming an executor takes more consideration than the automatic naming of one's spouse or eldest child. Successful planning calls for a great deal of reflection, foresight, and clear communication among all.

Today's estate requires a break from a tradition of narrowly focused secrecy, to a comprehensive, validating end-of-life plan.

. . .

Who was Terri Schiavo? —In 1990, at age 26, Terri collapsed from full cardiac arrest, leaving her in an irreversible persistent vegetative state. With no living will for guidance, a feeding tube was inserted, keeping her alive for fifteen years. After the first three years on life support, an ongoing court battle ensued between her husband and legal guardian, Michael Schiavo, who requested that Terri's feeding tube be removed, and her parents, Robert and Mary Schindler, who fought to keep her alive.

President G. W. Bush and his brother, Florida Governor Jeb Bush, became involved in the right-to-die case from 2003 to 2005. Adding to the chaos, the Vatican, anti-abortion groups, random protesters, and politicians such as House Majority Leader Tom DeLay joined the cause. Judge George Greer, who would decide the case, received death threats and was forced to make his final ruling in hiding.

Ultimately, Greer ordered the feeding tube removed, and Terri died two weeks later. An autopsy revealed her brain consisted of mostly spinal fluid and her optic nerves had deteriorated.

Hallways often symbolize the unconscious passageways through which people travel to either life or death. They also represent a new level of consciousness or a new experience, as well as a journey into the unknown.
       JAMES R. LEWIS, THE DREAM ENCYCLOPEDIA

• • •

Is it a vision, or a waking dream?
       JOHN KEATS, "ODE TO A NIGHTINGALE"

Waking Dreams

Day Four/Five: Each day and night has been the same. Dad sleeps only in fifteen-minute intervals, and then demands to be walked from the living room to the bathroom down the hall. He now prefers Step-mum's new mechanical-lift easy chair to his bed. Obviously, the chair is easy. More than anything, he hates being stuck away in the guest room. But it's a long, slow walk up the hall for a body shutting down, and for a body that's sleep deprived.

Sometime during the night, sitting on the hallway floor by the bathroom waiting to take him back, I think someone is handing me a fistful of silverware. It's so vivid I stretch out my arm and lean forward. The movement jerks me awake. It is unnerving to experience such vulnerability, to be blindsided by the need for sleep.

By 4:30 a.m., beyond physical exhaustion, my determination to keep watch collapses under the heavy weight of predawn silence. I fall asleep at the end of the sofa, wrapped in an itchy afghan that gives me coughing fits.

· · ·

Dad is trying to get up to make coffee. It is 6:00 a.m. I've no idea what occurred during the last hour and a half. What if he had tried to get up earlier and had fallen and I hadn't heard him? I must not fall asleep again.

I rise from the sofa, prepare the coffeemaker, and wait. Dad says he is ready for a little breakfast, but he doesn't know what he wants. Maybe some toast. I prepare toast. No, he doesn't want toast.

We have an appointment with his doctor today. The results of the MRI are in. We will find out whether or not the cancer has spread to his brain and is the source of his confusion.

I go to the bathroom to freshen up, knowing I won't be able to shower again, but manage to wash my face and brush my teeth before Dad yells, "All right! That's enough! I need help!"

I rush out, afraid he has fallen. He is shouting from the chair, demanding to be walked to the bathroom. I help him dress and worry about the twenty-minute drive on the highway and the drive through town. What if I am once more thrown into sleep while driving? Step-mum has arranged for someone else to drive her and Dad. But I am determined I will not be left in the dark this time. I need to understand what is happening to Dad. I need to understand what I am supposed to do and what he needs.

I back out of the driveway and straight into the fence. My reflexes, it seems, are sluggish. I take a deep breath and carefully, so very carefully, drive into town.

ADAPTED FROM JOURNAL ENTRIES, MAY 1997

The doctor was straightforward. No, the cancer had not spread to Dad's brain. The cancer was, however, ravaging his liver. The treatments were no longer working. Nothing more could be done. Speaking in a tone that felt more like chitchat than a declaration, he did not cause us panic.

We did not question. We did not cry.

Dad would have to be admitted to the hospital, the doctor said. I later found out this decision was made based on the doctor's visit after seeing me. The doctor didn't think I could hold up much longer, so he was giving me a break. With doc's orders in hand, we drove to the hospital in silence.

After completing the admissions process, we were sent upstairs to the oncology ward. Dad and I sat across the overcrowded waiting room from one another. I marveled that during this entire morning of doctor's office waiting and hospital waiting, he had not once requested to use the restroom. He sat calm, in total contradiction to everything we had gone through during the past four days and nights. There was no agitation. There were no demands. In my exhausted condition, I started thinking I had imagined everything. How else to explain his sudden ability to sit there—and behave?

After another hour or so of waiting for a room to become available, Dad smiled a perky smile and asked, "How about checking on Mother?"

"On who?" I asked, wondering if he was becoming confused again. I had never heard him refer to Step-mum as "Mother." *She's not my mother*, I wanted to say.

"On Mother," he repeated.

"You mean Step-mum?"

"Yes. Yes," he answered in a serious tone, his enthusiasm fading.

I was reluctant to leave before he was settled into a room. What if he needed something? What if he became unreasonably confused, or lost? On the other hand, I could not reason him out of his sudden concern about "Mother." I cornered a nurse and instructed her about Dad's random confusion, his frequent requests to use the restroom, and his need for assistance with walking. She said not to worry. I did anyhow.

Step-mum sat downstairs in the common waiting area, having declared that she was no longer able to stand up, let alone walk. I asked how she was doing.

She said she needed to go home, "Now!"

Back upstairs, Dad said he was fine, and I should go ahead and take her home.

The nurse said he would be fine, for me to go home, as well. Go home and sleep. Nurse's orders.

It didn't feel right to leave him alone in a room filled with strangers on the day he was told—without being told—he was dying.

Or does leaving really not matter, because I am already sleeping, dreaming another silverware dream? Soon to awake, sitting in the hallway, waiting on Dad.

Sleep deprivation can be dangerous and cause problems with memory and concentration, irritability, susceptibility to infection, problem-solving ability, and at its extreme can lead to death. Studies have concluded even less than six hours sleep a night can affect coordination, reaction time, and judgment. Sleep deprivation has also been found to trigger sleepwalking episodes in people who are genetically predisposed to sleepwalking.

As a caregiver, be good to yourself, demand help, find support.

Can I Get a Witness?

> *The very fact that you have lawsuits among you means you have been completely defeated already.*
>
> 1 CORINTHIANS 6:7

According to its date, Dad's will was drawn up after the doctor told us that the treatments were no longer working. It was signed on the third morning during that last hospital stay, less than two weeks before he died.

I know he was confused during this time and had even been placed in restraints the first night. When I discovered him tied to the bed, I located his nurse and demanded we hire a full-time sitter instead.

"He can only have a sitter if he is a danger to himself or to anyone else," she told me.

"If he isn't a danger to himself or to anyone else," I asked, "then why the restraints?"

She ordered a sitter.

I'll never forget how empty and broken he appeared. When we finally learned about the will, and I held a copy in my hand, memories of his brokenness flashed before me. I noted his signatures grew weaker on each page of the seven-page document, and I wondered what that morning had been like for him.

Who was with him that morning? Who were the witnesses?

Obviously, during the time the will is actually brought out and used, the testator is no longer available for comment. So, the witness serves as a legal tool to prove that the testator: (1) really did sign the will, (2) wasn't loony *while signing* the will, and (3) was not forced into signing the will.

The witness cannot be a beneficiary or related to the testator. Either of these situations could cause the will to be contested. Therefore, the witness is usually a stranger. Some law firms use their office staff, in which case the witness may have a casual frame of reference toward the testator. But a witness could also be an absolute stranger from the hallway.

Whoever the required two (or three) witnesses are, the key word here is stranger. And the key question becomes: during the moment it takes to witness the signing of a will document, how can a *stranger* adequately determine the testator is of sound mind?

Being unfamiliar with family circumstances, how can an outsider assess the testator has not been pressured into signing the will document by those whom he depends upon for care? How can they make a reliable, two-minute evaluation that the testator understood what was happening?

Human nature being what it is, wouldn't most people asked to witness a will, do so without question?

Dad's off-and-on lucidity amazed me during those final days. In a *snap*! he was coherent; then *snap*! a blank slate. A testator can bounce between knowing what is happening and not knowing what is happening. As long as the testator signed the will "during a lucid moment" and the signing was properly witnessed and absent of coercion, the will is deemed valid.

To (hopefully) prevent a legal challenge, a testator can ask his doctor to verify that—yes, indeed—he has enough sound mind left to sign his own will.

However, will contests really aren't that common. Undue influence and state-of-mind challenges are difficult and costly to prove. Also, a successful contest might not benefit the heirs at all because it would negate the current will, thereby causing the estate to become intestate. This would mean the estate (if anything is left after the court battle) would be distributed to the *legal heirs* according to state intestate law.

Think through your situation to determine whether a successful contest would be worth its weight in despair. Compare outcomes between the current will distribution arrangement and a forced intestate distribution.

When settling an estate, if the events that led up to or surrounded the signing of the will are in question, ask your attorney to locate and interview the testator's doctor and the witnesses. If it serves no other purpose, a little investigating can go a long way toward allowing your sound mind to rest.

. . .

Some things to consider:
- If you died without a will, who would be your legal heirs according to your state's intestate laws?
- According to state law exactly what and how much of your estate would each heir receive?
- What is the "age of majority" in your state?
- Who are the "issues" (the children and grandchildren) of your heirs or beneficiaries?

The Meant to Do List

> *When we talk about the ways in which a man can die, we forget about the absence of faith.*
>
> — Source Unknown

Dad sat on the edge of his hospital bed, head hung low, staring at the floor. Silent. Who would have thought asking the question would be so difficult? It had come to me easily enough. Just a little something that should be asked. It shouldn't be that big of a deal. Really.

Still, the question gripped my mind. I was fearful of what his reaction might be if the words were let loose and bounced about the room—words implying the "D" word, as in "dying." Now and then I would try to force the question out anyhow, but it held on tight. So, my mind split in two, took sides—logic against emotion—and wrestled with the situation.

At last, I blurted, "Dad, do you have a minister you would like to speak with?"

Slowly he raised his head to meet my eyes. It was clear the words had not frightened him at all. To the contrary, they seemed to have raised him up, filled him with light.

"Yes!" He beamed. "Oh, but I can't remember his name."

He thought and thought. I was astonished. And relieved. Asking had definitely been the right thing to do.

"Is there someone I could call who might know?"

With the gesturing of a fidgety child, he instructed me to look up the number of a mutual friend. Thankfully, his friend answered and was able to provide me with the minister's name, as well as his number. Dad would have been terribly disappointed, and it would have been a very long night if we had been unable to make immediate contact.

The minister said he would be happy to stop by the next morning.

Dad eased back onto the bed pillows, now cocooned by peace of mind.

"OK. What do we need to do next?" he asked, unexpectedly eager for task.

I looked over at the living will form on the table. Yep, it was still there. Untouched. *We'll talk about that one tomorrow. I just can't think about it tonight. Not yet.*

"I don't know." I shrugged. "I don't know what we need to do next."

We found the minister. Dad was eager to see him. For the first time in days, he was smiling, relaxed. We did good.

We never got around to anything else.

It is as natural to die as to be born; and to a little infant, perhaps the one is as painful as the other.

FRANCIS BACON, ESSAYS 1625

In the In-between

> *While the Sumerians expected to endure eternity in the gloom of the House of Dust, the ancient Egyptians envisaged a brighter future, linking the afterlife to the sun.*
>
> — John Ashton and Tom Whyte, The Quest for Paradise: Visions of Heaven and Eternity in the World's Myths and Religions

There was a healing going on in the room across the hall. The sound of a man's voice—loud, determined, and punctuated by sporadic shouts of "Amen!"—had drowned out Dad's show on TV. I caught a glimpse of the group standing behind a partially drawn curtain. And then I closed Dad's door. That's when the guilt seeped in underneath, tracing my path back to the chair near the foot of his bed. *Had I shut out—turned my back upon—a miracle?*

Exactly when, in this age of control, is it acceptable to say *when*? To rest assured that we are in fact human and limited? When is it acceptable to allow the dying to die without being tugged upon?

The tragedy of life, it is said, *is not that it ends so soon, but that we wait so long to begin it.* (Anonymous) But what is so soon? What is enough?

We celebrate the fighters. Those who are willing to suffer, endure, beat the odds, survive, and win the race. Those who always refused to let go and those who fought valiantly to the very end but lost. We are in love with stories of struggle for what they provide: the made-for-TV movies, evoking goose-bumpy moments of inspired strength. But the moments fade; we move on. We forget. So, we adorn our wrists with brightly colored plastic bands lest we forget to struggle and to survive.

We admonish the wimps for having lived badly. Despite accomplishments, despite having been good, decent people, to some they are unworthy of the story. They are the footnotes: *He smoked. He drank. I told her to exercise. He wouldn't lose weight. She refused to go to the doctor. He refused chemo. She hid cigarettes in her closet, in shoeboxes!* Tsk, tsk. We shake our heads.

If only, we delude, *they might have lived on forever.* But truth is, we don't do forever on earth.

So here we are, and I have to ask: *What is the purpose of this in-between time? A test of faith?* Are we really being challenged to raise our voices in unison, beseeching last-minute miracles in hospital rooms? He who has the most faith wins? Or is this the chrysalis stage of life, where "the caterpillar is almost completely broken down into a soup of cells before the butterfly becomes built up." * A necessary process, and a miracle as well.

---

*An Obsession with Butterflies, by Sharman Apt Russell.

Imagine if each time the caterpillar anchored itself to a secure spot—readied itself to shed its skin, to harden into pupa—we reached out and plucked it, just because we could. Or what if we chose instead to circle round, holding hands, praying for the caterpillar to remain a caterpillar? Would our prayer be born of faith? Or born of fear? And if it is born of fear, where is our faith? Would the prayer be for the caterpillar or for us?

Respect the process, contend against death, or pray for a healing? Heavenly Father knows best. Let go. Let God. For everything there is a season. And a purpose to every reason. Have faith. Chin up. Not nice to fool Mother Nature. Peace.

Who's in Charge Here?

After two years of battling cancer, it was obvious he would not last long. Dad was sent home from the hospital to die.

When the doctor consulted me about home healthcare arrangements, I did not hesitate to order hospice as well as a full-time nurse. I wasn't comfortable going back into Dad's house alone. From my point of view, the situation there was too unpredictable and too bizarre. I wanted someone neutral in the home at all times.

Under the circumstances, I believed that was the best arrangement for everyone involved. I soon discovered, however, I had no say in the matter. Dad's wife, who still maintained she could no longer walk, and had confined herself to bed, was in charge. I was told she would not allow hospice into the home and had balked at hiring help.

At the time I had no idea how hospice worked or what it cost or what were other cost-related details of Dad's care. I did know he had excellent health insurance coverage, as well as a supplement. I knew the slightest extra expense would still be an issue, but I also knew Dad did not have long to live, and he could afford whatever the extra cost would be.

Besides, what else could possibly matter now? I could never understand people who worried about expense at the end, people who worried over hiding the money and saving the money. Why should a person sweat and skimp and save and plan for seventy-three years, only to sacrifice comfort at the end? Why not afford a comfortable ending to a life of thrift?

· · ·

To the Bitter End—A conservatorship lawsuit over the care of a loved one can be time consuming, and both emotionally and financially costly. Second marriages are highly susceptible to guardianship battles between the second spouse and the adult children of a first marriage. Encourage cooperation and communication among the people in your life. The deeper the wounds dividing your family, the more care and honest reflection is needed in end-of-life planning.

. . .

Long-term Health Care is another important topic to explore *before* a crisis. Learn what type of end-of-life care would be available to you and at what cost. Then discuss with your entire family what accommodations you would prefer. Above all, be clear about who you have placed in charge of your health-care decisions, should the need arise. Again, this is a good time to learn of the wishes and expectations of family and friends regarding their own end-of-life plan.

Get to know your local hospice and what services they offer to patients and the community. In the process, you may even become a hospice volunteer or a financial donor. Whatever the outcome, I'm certain you will feel comfort just knowing they are there.

. . .

Nevermore

But the raven, sitting lonely on the placid bust, spoke only / That one word, as if his soul in that one word he did outpour . . . / Then the bird said, "Nevermore."

EDGAR ALLAN POE, THE RAVEN

Somehow the days leading up to Dad's hospital stay had continued to flow, despite the silence and the not talking and the incessant tick, tick, ticking of the schoolhouse clock hanging on the wall above his chair.

Step-mum had warned that Dad was jittery because of the medication he was on, and he was unable to tolerate sound of any sort, especially TV or music—or even laughter. I was told they had to let a visiting nurse go because she laughed too much. I tried to abide with the golden rule, spending each hour upon hour in silence, except for the maddening tick of the raven clock and its quarterly chime.

One night I concluded the chiming had to be the cause of Dad's fifteen-minute routine, so I removed the clock's batteries during one of our bathroom visits. What I hadn't realized was his obsessive reliance upon the clock. Nor that he was desperately and silently trying to make sense of how we came to such a sorry state, frozen in time.

But the fifteen-minute routine continued, anyhow. Dad eventually asked about the clock, and I was told to put the batteries back in. So, we compromised. Dad got to keep his obsession. But I located the volume control and turned off the chime.

Desperate for something—*anything*—to distract us, I finally got up the nerve to ask if there wasn't some favorite music of Dad's to listen to or a favorite video to watch. He thought for a bit and decided on a video of *River Dance*, such an obvious wrong choice on so many levels. Still we made the attempt. We lasted about five minutes and that was that.

· · ·

Music can help take the edge off of endless doctor's office visits, medical treatments, and replace homebound obsessing with relaxation and comfort, as well as aid with pain management. Set up a mobile, easy-to-access assortment of favorite tunes for both patient and caregiver. Find out what types of music therapy are available through the local hospice or community.

Laughter and music can be the best medicine when given the chance. Indulge!

· · ·

Recommended reading—*The Mozart Effect: Tapping the Power of Music to Heal the Body, Strengthen the Mind, and Unlock the Creative Spirit* by Don Campbell.

· · ·

Hospice and Other Earthly Angels

hos' pice, n.—a place of refuge for travelers
WEBSTER'S NEW UNIVERSAL UNABRIDGED DICTIONARY,
DELUXE SECOND EDITION, 1983 AND 1955.

All too often the end-of-life traveler becomes lost to a time over-shadowed by mental and physical exhaustion, delusion and confusion, turmoil and chaos for all. Instead, the final journey should be an opportunity for reflection, clarification, and the sharing of memories. A chance to validate one's time spent on earth. Most of all, and as much as possible, the traveler should be provided a shelter of continuous physical and emotional comfort. Friends and family should have access to a constant, reliable source of information, reassurance, and support.

This is where hospice comes in.

"Hospice is the voice of reason," my sister, Connie, a former hospice nurse, explained to me during a phone interview. "Everybody has to die. How they die becomes the most important question. Every patient wants to be comfortable."

Hospice care is offered to the patient who has six months or fewer to live. This does not mean the patient will die within six months or has to die within six months. It is merely a guideline. Care can be extended beyond this time. The patient, family, or the physician may request hospice as soon as a terminal prognosis has been made, but a doctor's referral is required.

At that point, the emphasis changes from cure to comfort and care. Hospice staff will meet with the family, the patient, and the physician(s) to discuss available services and to create a plan of individualized care. Questions regarding insurance coverage and payment requirements are addressed.

A medical social worker will help the patient fill out and sign the paperwork needed to accept hospice. Advance Directives, including the Do Not Resuscitate order, may or may not be considered during enrollment, depending upon whether the patient and family might need more time to adjust to the situation. Although patients are encouraged to complete these documents to make their wishes clear, they are not required to do so.

Hospice should be thought of as a resource, not as a sitting service.

Most hospice patients wish to receive care and to die at home, and the majority actually does. Families with an extreme amount of conflict might choose to place the patient in a hospice facility, but this situation is rare.

A hired home-caregiver is usually a sitter, not a nurse. Statistically, family, friends, and volunteers provide 90 percent of day-to-day care, with a hospice nurse available by phone, 24/7, to answer questions and offer support. Frequency of staff visits depend on individual need and are adjusted accordingly. On average, the hospice nurse, an RN specifically trained to care for the dying, spends one hour per visit, and the hospice aide spends one to two hours per visit with each patient. A patient's care team might include doctors, nurses, hospice aides, social workers, chaplains, bereavement specialists and trained volunteers.

Patient comfort and dignity are always priorities. Necessary medications will be administered in the home, and there will be clear guidelines for their use. The hospice nurse is trained to assess and anticipate potential problems of increased pain and restlessness, and the need for extra assistance.

Spiritual needs are a priority, as well. Volunteer religious coordinators are available to come to the home, to read the Bible or other religious texts, or to just sit with the patient. Ongoing bereavement counseling is extended to family members.

While most families are able to put their differences aside during this time, some conflicts, unfortunately, run too deep. But hospice volunteers and professionals are aware of the dynamics within each family and will not exclude any family member. Family is encouraged to talk to the patient about unresolved issues and, most importantly, to seek forgiveness. The family is also encouraged to let the patient know that it is okay to leave this earth. Connie stressed, "Hospice is the voice of reason that says, at some point, you have to stop torturing yourself."

The end-of-life information provided by hospice staff is invaluable during this stressful, scary time. The caregiver will be informed about what specific physical symptoms to expect as death nears, such as paused or rattled breathing, or mottling, where the toes and fingers turn blue to black. Instruction and support with things that aren't immediately apparent, such as learning how to properly change an adult's diaper, and the resulting embarrassment and privacy issues, are acknowledged and addressed.

Hospice buffers the shock of the unknown.

• • •

Your Local Hospice May Provide:

- Assistance in care for a patient's physical, emotional, and spiritual needs, either at the patient's home, nursing home, assisted living facility, or hospice facility.
- Information and a support system available 24/7 for family and caregivers.
- Family caregiver training.
- **Respite care**—the hospice patient may be eligible for inpatient care up to five days, provided only "on an occasional basis," giving the caregiver a break.

Bereavement support programs—many hospices serve the community as a grief resource center. Programs offered through your local hospice, church, or community-sponsored resources might include:

- Individual bereavement counseling
- Grief and loss support groups for surviving:
  * Children
  * Teens
  * Adults (as parent, sibling, or grandparent)
- Survivors of suicide support group
- Surviving spouse support group
- Breast-cancer survivor counseling program
- Children's grief camp
- Crisis intervention counseling for businesses following a death in the workplace, layoffs and downsizing, and other traumatic events.

Pet loss counseling—the loss of a family pet is often a child's first experience with death. Pet counseling can help a parent or guardian explain the loss to a child or provide comfort to adults of any age. Veterinary hospice and in-home euthanasia are becoming a popular option and may offer grief related services.

• • •

Available therapies in your area that are used with pain and stress management, might include one or more of the following:
- Pet therapy
- Aromatherapy
- Music therapy
- Water therapy
- Reminiscence or life review therapy
- Massage therapy
- Therapeutic touch
- Writing and art therapy

Education, training and presentations on hospice care and related topics may also be available to the community and through local clubs and organizations. Contact your local hospice, American Red Cross, or AARP for more detailed information on free caregiver training and support programs. The AARP website provides a wealth of valid information on end-of-life topics.

• • •

Palliative care is a relatively new, holistic approach to pain management and symptom relief in patients with chronic or life-threatening illness. Its goal is to enrich the patient's quality of life so the patient may live as productive a life as possible.

Care is team oriented, focused on the whole person, not just the disease, while providing a support system that addresses the individual needs of the patient and their family. A team may include physicians, nurses, pharmacists, social workers, religious counselors, physical therapists, occupational therapists, music therapists, art therapists, and specially trained volunteers.

Care may be provided at a doctor's office, health clinic, long-term care setting, hospital, or the patient's home.

Unlike hospice care, palliative care may begin at any stage of illness and in conjunction with life-prolonging treatments such as chemotherapy, radiation, and surgery. The palliative approach neither hastens nor postpones death, but rather seeks to affirm life while regarding death as a normal process.

Palliative care is often referred to as "comfort care."

And life is eternal; and love is immortal; and death is only a horizon; and a horizon is nothing save the limit of our sight.
ROSSITER WORTHINGTON RAYMOND

Flight

I was too afraid to be alone with, or to be near to, my own father while he died. Afraid of Step-mum down the hall. Can you imagine? I sat across the room and held a long, one-sided, mental conversation with him, complaining about how stupid this was.

Nobody had given me a heads up—*hey, your father is dying, you might want to be here.* When I arrived, Step-mum's nurse friend was sitting with Dad. She told me he had been in a coma since morning, and she was surprised he hadn't passed away hours ago. At any rate, his time was near. It would happen soon. She needed to leave but said she would drop by again later. If there were anything I needed to say to him, I should say it now.

There was no need to say anything, I reassured myself smugly, *because Dad would know everything—anyhow—soon. On the other side.* And besides, this was his mess, and I didn't need to be the one to do any straightening out. All that mattered, as far as I was concerned, was for Dad to pass away in a peaceful environment. No anger/hurt/disappointment allowed.

Opening the door to a conversation of 'things that needed to be said' would only invite resentment inside. Next thing I knew, my hostility toward the woman confined to bed up the hall shoved its ugly way through, and I was sitting across the room, rehashing with Dad, ESP-style.

Freezing and nervous and shaking, I sought refuge outside in the warm desert air to smoke and await the arrival of Dad's caregiver (whom Step-mum had been forced to hire). I hated this middle-of-nowhere place. Dad and Step-mum chose to live upon these desolate grounds because they hated having neighbors. They detested being available for people to drop in or stop by. Together, they worshiped isolation.

Dad chose this spot to build his home, miles from town, and more miles down horrid washboard roads that were impassable during gully-washer rainstorms and invisible during sandstorms. The land directly across from the house was Bureau of Land Management property. A barbed wire fence and two mammoth driveway gates buffered this four-acre home on the open range from rogue cattle and rogue people. Dad and Step-mum lived as secluded a life as possible.

And then, they needed people to stop by. A lot of people. Daily.

Far, far away, across the distant valley, I caught sight of the circling of a bird—a hawk, perhaps? Entranced by the motion, I watched the creation of each purposeful, heavenly sphere bring her mile upon mile closer. Circle entwined in elegant circle, she floated her way upon the heavy, pristine blue sky—a comforting display of grace.

Somehow, I had understood from first sight that we were directly upon her path. When she finally did arrive, I saw she was, indeed, a hawk. She circled once, twice, directly overhead as an unease settled in me. Had she come for Dad? Was his spirit to sail away upon those majestic wings?

She drifted once more above the land, and then journeyed on, all the while surveying the earth beneath her. I hurried inside, stopped short in the doorway. Dad inhaled one long breath—exhaled that long breath—and his breath was gone. Without moving, without taking my eyes off of him, I panic-yelled for Step-mum's daughter as he again struggled to inhale.

"I thought he had stopped breathing," I blurted in awkward apology and denial.

She walked over to the bedside and issued an unexpected, boisterous demand, "Come on, Casey. Breathe! Breathe!"

Kaleidoscope tides of sickly yellows rushed over him, receded as he struggled to obey, and then rolled back in ashen gray.

Why was she calling him back? Why was she demanding he stay? I could not comprehend this insult upon his body. I closed my eyes, wishing *her* away. I wished I could take hold of his hand, guide him to the hawk angel, and assure him it was time to go. That he should set sail upon wings of air and spirit and light, and--

The front door opened. I greeted Leo, my husband, from where I stood with an urgent, silent plea to make the daughter stop. *Please make her stop torturing my father!* Then everything seemed to pause at once, and with one last, deep breath—with a magician's flair—Dad's life, vanished before our eyes.

I wanted to look up—to wave. I would have, if we had been alone. I did so in my mind. I should have anyhow. Because Dad, who loved space and all its mysteries, who believed wholeheartedly that someday man would really be able to beam Scotty up, had—at last—embarked upon the ride of his eternal life.

Another disciple said to him, "Lord, first let me go and bury my father."

But Jesus told him, "Follow me, and let the dead bury their own dead."

Matthew 8:21-22

Going Home: A Place of Rest

My dilemma over whether or not to attend my own father's funeral had not only consumed my days but visited my nights as well.

I was, by the way, leaning toward not.

Is it a sin not to attend your father's funeral? I really didn't believe so. Dad wouldn't have believed so, although he was a faithful funeral attendee. He was a regular at the local funerals of friends and acquaintances and of friends and family far away.

He traveled 1,600 miles to attend the funeral of the twin sister of Connie's mother, Dad's first wife, even though she and Dad had divorced when Connie was a young child. At the time, his act of devotion baffled me. I remember thinking I couldn't imagine affording a vacation, let alone the expense of traveling to someone's funeral.

I was not invited to my grandmother's funeral in Kansas. I was not required to attend the funeral of my maternal grandmother in Oklahoma, mostly because I had already made two trips while she was ill, and most of all, I was broke. I had been required, however, to attend my mother's two funerals, despite begging Dad to not force me to attend the second one. Did I really need to fly back to Mom's hometown in Oklahoma for a second service? Wasn't the one in our hometown enough? But Dad was adamant—*My God, what would the townspeople think?*

So therein lies the rub: What *would* the townspeople think?

Yet, on that morning—the morning of Dad's funeral—I recalled a Bible chapter and verse that had entered my thoughts during the night. Exactly what this meant, I didn't know, but my mind played it over and over: Matthew 8:22 . . . Matthew 8:22.

The house was empty. Connie had asked Leo to drive her to a private viewing she arranged for herself, because her attempt to attend the viewing the previous night had been a fiasco. Apparently, Step-mum planted herself in Dad's wheelchair and parked at one end of his casket, a patronizing sight more than Connie could bear. So, she returned home, called the mortuary, and made her own arrangements.

Avoiding the subject of death and in search of normalcy, my daughter Shelley had spent the night at a friend's house. In the quiet, I took out one of my Bibles and located the verse that continued to float around in my head: "But Jesus told him, 'Follow me, and let the dead bury their own dead.'"

Wow! Isn't the subconscious mind totally amazing?

It seemed as though my problem was solved. And I had the Bible to back me up. *The* Bible, *The* Book, *The* Big Guy Himself was backing me up. Not attending your own father's funeral was obviously not a sin. God all but said so. Unfortunately, though, the townsfolk wouldn't know that. And although I was certain Jesus wouldn't give a hoot about what folks said, I settled on a different plan. My intention was to arrive just before the service began and to ease in somewhere toward the back. But you know what they say about plans—and about intentions.

I loved the commercial where a group of mourners, all clad in black, walked slowly behind a hearse easing along a country road. The priest looked nervously to the side, toward a lady wearing a red dress in the procession. A voice asked, "What is the color of defiance?"

I was the color of defiance.

Shelley and I arrived at the church to find Connie and a friend of Step-mum's standing in the entryway—waiting for us. Not only were *they* waiting for us, but also the entire event had been put on hold. I panicked not knowing what Connie had gone through. By the look on her face, it hadn't been pleasant.

"We're sitting in the back," I said.

"Oh, dear. At a time like this, you need family," Step-mum's friend responded.

Connie grabbed Shelley by an arm, grabbed me by an arm and declared, "We *are* family," triggering the lyrics "I got all my sisters with me," replacing the Bible verse in my mind.

We sat together in the back: Shelley and Connie and my father-in-law and me. A few days earlier, someone had called Leo asking if he and our son, Ryan, would serve as pallbearers. So, my two guys sat uncomfortably stiff in the front.

Finally, the other family walked up the aisle. One of the members of Step-mum's group shot us an unforgettable killer glare. Ouch! Most of what happened after that blurred as soon as it occurred, as though I suddenly had access to life's fast-forward and delete buttons. Then there were those moments just too good to trash.

Sadly, I didn't recognize most of the people in attendance. I realized several of Dad's friends had already passed, but I had expected to see more, and not so much of Step-mum's family (a family that travels to funerals). On the other hand, it's kind of difficult to recognize people from the back whom you haven't seen in years.

We didn't know the minister standing at the lectern. He wasn't the one Dad had asked me to call. This minister was Baptist. As it turned out, so was Step-mum. I apologize to any Baptists reading this, but frankly, my parents did not care for Baptists. I'm certain some folks would claim Dad had made a deathbed conversion—saved by the bell—Amen. Knowing Dad as I did, it simply verified his state of confusion during his final weeks.

The service began—blur, blur, blur. Then out of the blur, the minister, whom Dad had possibly not known until his last couple of weeks on earth and whom we had never met before, made an implied accusatory statement. Oddly, none of us had a precise recollection afterward of the wording. However, we were certain the words were meant to sting and as they were spoken, Step-mum's friend s-l-o-w-l-y turned her head our way and shot a damning look of "did you catch that?" I challenged her judgment eye-to-eye and startled her. She made an instant retreat.

The minister talked about what it meant to be there. How attending showed respect for Dad. I disagreed. It's all too easy to do things for show. You can show up with disrespect. You can respect without showing up. Pretense and false motive, heartbreak and disappointment line our insides, out of sight. That's why God said judging was His job, and His job only.

Still we judge.

Somewhere, in the midst of it all, a mystery woman's voice burst through the heavens and into song. I can't remember exactly what hymn it was, but God forgive me, it was horrid! With each nail-screeching-across-a-chalk-board note, it was all I could do to hold in laughter. Several times during the ordeal, I turned to Connie. She was absolutely stoical, refusing to share in those moments of irony. Her resolve made me want to laugh even more. But I managed to contain myself.

At least, I think I did.

Two limos sat parked outside. We didn't know if one had been intended for our family, or if both were for the other family and their kin. Connie went to her rental car to drive in the procession. At first, Leo, Shelley, and I were going to ride with Ryan and his family, but then we realized there wasn't enough room, and why weren't we riding with Connie, anyhow?

The procession had already circled its wagons, Connie among them. At last, as we walked through the parking lot into the conclave of automobiles filled with staring spectators, I lost my resolve in an instant of revelation. I was so tired of bizarre situations, of miscommunication, of suppressed communication, of pretense.

Then I remembered the part of Dad that loved a good joke, the part of him that loved a good laugh. This slapstick funeral service was the perfect testimony to Dad's life, after all. Struggling with a hybrid of teary-eyed emotions as we walked to Connie's car to hitch a ride to the cemetery, before townsfolk and God, I had to laugh, "Here's to you, Dad."

• • •

Silent Messengers

While driving in procession toward the cemetery, Connie found herself thinking about Dad's well-known fascination and obsession for roadrunners. She also began to question why, despite numerous visits to the Southwest, she had never seen one of those odd desert creatures.

"So many times when I talked to Dad on the phone," she recalled, "he would tell me he was watching a roadrunner at play in his yard, but I think he was just playing with me. I don't believe they exist."

Where could I possibly find a roadrunner to prove the reality, I wondered? In just a few hours Connie would be aboard a plane bound for home, and even if we had more time, I wasn't aware of any particular place where a roadrunner could be found. As far as I knew, one would have to find us.

The graveside ceremony was awkward and absent of comfort amid strangers who were, at least in my mind, rooting for Step-mum's team. I stood in the back with my own small clan and welcomed the distraction of meditations on how to find a roadrunner.

At last, the ceremony ended, and just as my family and I eased into the refuge of our cars, Shelley shouted, "Look over there!" Following her gesture toward the area where we had been standing, we were astonished to see—not one—but two roadrunners at play.

I turned to motion to Ryan and his family in the car behind us, but they were already transfixed by the sight. Then, as if on cue, the roadrunners stopped, turned and gazed in our direction, bidding us farewell.

For me, their miraculous presence spoke a simple, yet powerful message: Believe! God exists, roadrunners exist, and everlasting life exists. Wasn't it obvious? Connie would later confide that, for her, the messengers had delivered a much-needed validation and a much-needed chance to say goodbye.

Connie returned home and went to work immediately after Dad's service. Shelley and I journeyed north in search of sacred places and balance. At least that was my original plan. A teenage daughter doesn't necessarily make the best companion during a spiritual quest— especially one who is agnostic, who just lost her grandfather, and who is being forced to travel hundreds of miles from home to places she couldn't care less about seeing.

Besides, such an endeavor is more of a go-it-alone type of deal. So, we returned home to routine. We wadded up our grief, our hurt, and disappointment, stuffed them into pockets deep, and then went about our lives. There was no worry over who was getting what or who was doing what. There were no battles to be fought. With dignity intact, what we did not know could not hurt us. For the next two years—at least in respect to Dad's estate—we lived in ignorant bliss.

I'm not saying the silence didn't hurt. It would have been wonderful—perhaps might even have delivered closure—to have received a memento or a few words of encouragement reaching out from his grave. Terms of endearment.

We knew Dad had not been in control of his situation for a long time and the decisions made had not been his own, but the silence still hurt. It hurt big. So, I imagined there had been other plans, other intentions now lost to time and circumstance. I pretended Dad wanted to somehow communicate all of the things he always meant to say but didn't or couldn't—and all of those things were being kept from us.

I had to pretend. The alternative would have meant Dad had never cared.

An Unopened Gift of Hummingbirds

Is this the purpose of the butterfly?
To offer proof of what we know in our hearts but cannot see?

I overheard this little story shared between the office nurse and receptionist while waiting for my appointment. Apparently, the nurse had just returned to work after traveling to attend her father's funeral:

"My mother is having a horrible time. After the funeral, all of us were sitting on the front porch when, suddenly, a group of hummingbirds flew right up to us and, well, they just hovered. Mom jumped up and headed for the front door. Then she stopped, sat back down, and began sobbing. I asked what was wrong, and she said that my father loved hummingbirds so much. She said she was going inside the house to bring him out so he could see. And then she remembered. He was gone."

What a magical sight that must have been. Neither of the women suggested that the event had been a form of communication. At least not out loud. I wanted to reassure them that the display had been exactly that: an unopened gift of hummingbirds sent by the father. They were the means through which he could say, "Hey! Check this out. I'm doing great!" But I didn't.

I wanted to tell her about Dad and about his roadrunner messengers. But I didn't. Still, I hoped that the daughter, and especially her mother, eventually realized the significance of the gift.

In the early 1900s, psychiatrist Carl Jung was so convinced of such phenomena, he developed the concept of synchronicity, crediting Albert Einstein's theory of relativity as his inspiration. Years later, while examining the collective unconscious, Jung would encounter so many examples of synchronicity with such meaningful connections that, "their chance occurrence," he concluded, would be greatly improbable.

In *An Obsession with Butterflies*, author Sharman Apt Russell beautifully describes how winged inspiration, from the beginning of time, has been woven throughout various cultures' search for an eternal soul. Many different mythological accounts represent the souls of children, soldiers, or martyrs as butterflies. Jewish inmates carved butterflies into the walls of Polish concentration camps as symbols of resurrection: the wronged transformed to glorious flight.

When my mother passed away, I was not aware of such possibilities. Now I imagine she would have sent us butterflies, her favorite. Subtle and beautiful. Elegant kisses on wings. They would have been easy to miss on that warm spring day while we were grieving.

"They say our loved ones have trouble communicating when we are crying," recently offered an acquaintance. We had been discussing pets that died. It seems our pets communicate from beyond, as well.

How often do we shut out miracles by building a wall of grief? Or fail to recognize miracles when they come wrapped inside unexpected forms, simply because we take for granted the wondrousness of flight?

Many families have at least one leader, a matriarch or patriarch, who keeps the crew bonded and functioning through good times and times of crisis. Unfortunately, all too often, a family once united by a solid sense of unity breaks to pieces upon the death of this central figure. Holiday and family traditions dissolve and members who shared every step of their lives together and who could never imagine coming unglued, no longer make an effort to communicate.

Who represents your family glue? What can be done to ensure solidarity remains intact after they are gone?

Direction

> *I do beseech you to direct your efforts more to preparing youth for the path and less to preparing the path for youths.*
>
> Benjamin Lindsey

When the last parent dies, there is a radical shift in balance. Despite one's age, despite one's caregiving role, vulnerability creeps in alongside the loss. Then your entire universe collapses unto itself.

My half-sister Connie became an elder, and orphaned, in the same final breath. She had felt the burden and precariousness from the instant Dad passed away. Perhaps even before. The reality took longer for me. It came to me in snippets. In those mindless moments while thinking, "Oh, I'll call Dad and ask about that." Or while looking through the ads and spotting a coupon for Dad's brand of coffee—and then remembering: Dad is gone.

Becoming a family elder means looking down to discover that you are suddenly walking the tightrope of life without a safety net. No one is around to watch your back, to catch you when you fall. No one is left to turn to for advice or for direction. It's all up to you now.

You grasp your dilemma. Your breathing quickens, your mind races: Did I pay attention all those years, take sufficient notes? How much had I taken for granted, tossed aside along the way?

Have I prepared my own children for their life journey? Have I provided them with sufficient tools?

Will they know the dangers? Will they know the way?

Think not forever of yourselves, O Chiefs, nor of your own generation.

Think of continuing generations of our families, think of our grandchildren and of those yet unborn whose faces are coming from beneath the ground.

SPOKEN BY PEACEMAKER, FOUNDER OF THE IROQUOIS CONFEDERACY, CIRCA CE 1,000

Kindred

Heritage Street, part of the Clark County Museum in Henderson, Nevada, is a tree-lined nostalgic lane of restored homes ranging in dates beginning in the 1890s— all open to the public. My granddaughter, Kat, and I refer to this area as our Mayberry, USA. It is our favorite place in the entire world to go back to.

On this day, I have brought my childhood friend, Judy, who is visiting from out of town.

It is a lukewarm day in April, definitely not cold and not too hot, but hot enough. So, we take time between houses to rest on sidewalk benches and front porch steps. We sit, talk, and allow the energies of the past to wrap us in memories of the timeless spring days and lavish green lawns of our youth. With clichéd reverence, we long for a once-upon-a-simpler-Heritage-Street time.

Each house is decorated, inside and out, with the furnishings and household items of its era. Judy and I behave like overgrown children tramping through exaggerated dollhouses, peering into every room, eager to search out the familiar.

I spot my grandmother's "good dishes" in kitchen cupboards. We wrack our brains for details. *What are the dishes called? Something-ware. Franciscan Ware! Desert Rose pattern. Made in? California! Judy's family had the Apple Pattern. Look! My grandmother had those very same fish hanging on her bathroom wall. Remember this green paint? This awful green paint. And look at that blond-wood furniture in the living room? Remember?*

Remember?

It is comforting to rediscover these old, familiar things. Even more, we find comfort in the implied: a time of values, more respect, less clutter. And yes, I do realize that I'm being a tad forgiving and sentimental. The decades also represent a time in our country of continuing great prejudices, male dominance, and fiercely guarded family sins. But it was also a time when, as a society, we were so close to finding a middle way. So close to understanding and enlightenment, when suddenly, somebody, somewhere got in an awful big hurry, skipped right over Nirvana, and plunged straight into comfy excess and greed.

Flash forward to a quiet April afternoon on a street made of make-believe with a distant view of one of the most excessive cities on earth—Las Vegas. Judy and I are sitting on a bench outside the restored print shop when the sound of enthusiastic chatter diverts our attention. (What can a nosy neighbor do but listen?) Up the street, a family of five—three young, school-aged boys, a grandmother, and a grandfather—are walking from one house to another.

"What did my mother always say?" the man cheerfully quizzes the boys. "What is our family motto?"

"Use it up, wear it out, make it work, or do without," they all chant.

I'm intrigued by this family with a motto. When they finally stroll our way, we all smile, nod, and exchange *hellos* because this is what you do on the streets of Mayberry. Time is forgiving here.

We chat with the grandparents and we learn they own two homes, one in California and a farm in another state, and they are on their annual vacation with the grandsons. They ask for suggestions of nearby places of history to explore. Yes, they already took the train ride in Boulder City last year, and they are considering the Grand Canyon for next year. The youngest boy groans with disapproval.

I admire the couple for their enthusiastic gifts to the boys of time and direction. For their gift of searching out and teaching the way things used to be. For their teaching of survival and for their giving of pure legacy.

As we part ways, I recall a recent newspaper article about how an entire fishing village of Thai sea gypsies survived the 2004 Asian tsunami by fleeing to a temple in the mountains. They had recognized the warning signs of the tsunami—not by experience—but through generations of stories preserved and presented to them by their elders.

Other fishermen, who had not received the gift of the past, saw a tantalizing opportunity rather than a threat when the waters receded. Lured by the sight of an abundance of fish lying exposed on the seabed, they themselves were baited and then trapped by the ferocious waves that rushed back in.

That is the danger of cushy times, of times of excess, of impersonal or scattered tribes. Why in the midst of unprecedented flood, death, and the most primal conditions that existed during Katrina's destruction of New Orleans was a man on the evening news shown wading waste-high through water, carrying a big-screen TV as if it were necessary to his survival.

Generations who have not known danger and sacrifice, and who have not been challenged, find difficulty in recognizing the signs on their own. And elders, who have settled into the comfort and have forgotten, have locked up the life jackets and thrown away the keys.

And then (as Alice afterwards described it) all sorts of things happened in a moment... in the dreadful confusion that was beginning.

LEWIS CARROLL, THROUGH THE LOOKING-GLASS AND WHAT ALICE FOUND THERE

In the Beginning, Dreadful Confusion That Was

The attorney was late, running behind schedule on that peculiar day of riddles. I waited in the reception area, pretending to read but instead preoccupied by thoughts of the unknown, known to be lurking somewhere in another room.

I made this appointment after receiving an out-of-the-blue phone call informing me that Step-mum had just passed away, two years after Dad, and after overhearing town gossip about Dad's will. Thanks to that gossip, we learned that a will existed, and that Dad's estate was in probate.

Closing his estate was something that I assumed needed to be done and had imagined it wouldn't be all that complicated. Having arrived with plenty of time to think, I was no longer certain, for a looming sense of dread had drifted in, filtering through the stale office air. Something wasn't right.

At last, with apology and nervous haste, the assistant led me inside a bleak conference room and seated me in a chair at midpoint of the long table. She chose a spot for herself at a distance from my right and immediately prepared for notetaking. The attorney sat down across from me.

"That is your father's estate," the attorney declared, motioning to my left, down toward the far end of the table. Dad's estate, as he implied, consisted of perhaps less than a half-dozen mystery papers of various sorts, resting loosely face-down on the table's corner.

Very peculiar. That Dad's estate would be all the way over there. At the end of the table.

All that way, away from us. Facing down so I cannot see.

A Riddle of Representation—Widower (A) and divorcée (B) marry. Afterward, an attorney creates a separate will for each. When spouse (A) dies, the attorney appoints surviving spouse (B) personal representative and trustee to his estate. However, (B) does not fulfill the duties of personal representative or trustee and dies a few years later, before the estate is closed.

The estates of (A) and (B) have been commingled.

The attorney appoints daughter of (B) personal representative to her mother's estate, as well as trustee to the estate of (A). He then appoints daughter of (A) alternate personal representative to her father's estate.

Question: Exactly whom does the attorney represent?

Answer: The attorney should avoid this situation altogether due to conflict of interest.

There are no guarantees in estate planning. However, by allowing yourself time to find a qualified legal guide and to make informed, thoughtful decisions, your chance for a successful transition can only increase.

• • •

Confused and Conflicted—The same attorney who created Dad's will also represented Dad's estate. Additionally, he created a will for Dad's wife, ultimately representing her estate. The day I stepped forward to claim my position as Dad's personal representative, I was not thinking "conflict of interest." Yet I somehow understood it was essential for the two commingled estates to divide, and I made the decision to retain an attorney of my choice. Although that decision would cost me the next three years of my life, I wouldn't have otherwise been provided the opportunity to locate any of Dad's assets.

Couples should coordinate their estate plans (including up-dates) for many reasons. But even the best of couples—especially those in a second or third marriage with children from any previous marriage(s)—should consider the advantages of securing separate representation.

Be aware, however, that the coordinated plan is not carved in stone. Either spouse may amend or replace his or her own will at any time with or without the knowledge or the consent of the other, which thereby affects the plan.

Most financial and estate-planning authorities do not recommend joint wills.

• • •

The Estate

> [A]nd those laws go hardly far enough that say simply, as to individual executors and testamentary trustees, that they are disqualified if they are infants, idiots, or habitual drunkards.
>
> EARL S. MACNEIL, MAKING THE MOST OF YOUR ESTATE; A GUIDE FOR THE SALARIED MAN (1957)

My family and I were shocked to learn that an unsupervised probate could dissolve into time without ever being closed; and that it was quite possible for the executor of an estate or his attorney to file the initial paperwork, receive the letters of appointment, and never file anything else; and that the executor might be able to act on an estate's behalf indefinitely, cash in assets, file taxes, *not* notify the heirs of their inheritance, or even comply with the instructions for distribution.

By law, estate executors are *required* to fulfill their duties and abide by the will. If they are unable or unwilling to fulfill those duties, they are *required* to step down. However, if they choose not to fulfill their duties, not to follow the will's instructions, and refuse to give up their position, the estate's attorney isn't allowed to squeal.

The attorney cannot assist in anything illegal and must warn the executor about what might happen—such as lawsuits or criminal penalties—as a result of their intentional defiance, but he must not tattle. The best the attorney can do is to red flag the judge by requesting to be removed from the case, but I was told this rarely happens.

One would assume the estate's attorney would represent the estate or, in a way, serve as the executor's boss. But thanks to a confidentiality attorney/client ethics rule, that isn't the case. Once the executor has been appointed, the attorney represents that executor over and above the estate. That was the most difficult fact for Connie and me to grasp. The true test comes when the executor realizes the position and power he holds.

...

Executor Privilege

Executor—the person named in a will, and approved by the court, to handle all the baggage left behind by the deceased.

Personal representative—another name for executor.

The basic checklist of executor duties—just a few simple lines of direction—appeared harmless:
- Petition court to open probate and admit the will
- Notify heirs and creditors
- Gather up assets
- Pay taxes
- Pay debts and estate expenses
- Distribute assets
- Petition court to close estate

Heck, Dad's estate had already been in probate for over two years. I was certain half of the duties were no longer relevant. *Piece of cake*, I thought.

My attorney warned that an executor needs thick skin. *Not a problem.* (No joke—I literally thought, *not a problem.*) You see, I imagined that we would be provided with everything we needed to know about Dad's estate. That I would meet with the family of Dad's wife and together we would sort through and figure out what inside the house belonged to whom. Then I would clean and fix up Dad's house, place it on the market, and when sold, I would do what needed to be done in order to close probate.

No problem.

I declared I would "as quickly and efficiently as possible, close the estate." (Yes, these were my exact words.) Instead, as Dad would have said, All hell broke loose. During the next three years I would tend to a multitude of unimagined tasks, including, but by no means limited to:

- Going to all local financial institutions and stockbrokers in search of Dad's accounts and safe deposit box
- Filing Dad's death certificate on his property at County Clerk's Office (required *upon the death of an owner*)
- Arranging for access onto Dad's property; making arrangements with sheriff's office to escort assistants and me onto property
- Spending sleepless nights trying to understand what Dad expected me to do, what Dad had intended, what the wording in his will meant
- Keeping a notebook documenting every single estate-related detail for backup, especially because the situation was precarious and hostile
- Petitioning court for access into Dad's house to list remaining personal property assets
- Arranging for witness to assist me onto property to take inventory

- Paying estate expenses out-of-pocket because there were no available estate funds
- Climbing through an unlocked back window to change locks after house was vacated
- Checking status of homeowner's insurance; learning that current policy would be cancelled because house was vacant
- Searching in a panic for new insurance (paying a very high rate because house was vacant.)
- Handling a multitude of household-related tasks including: hiring electrician to inspect house wiring; renting dumpster for property; locating estate appraiser; renting storage shed; finding real estate agent; distinguishing what of the remaining personal property belonged to which estate (separate property, community property); meeting with the family of Dad's wife to hand over residual items left on property belonging to her estate; listing these items; listing remaining items belonging to Dad's estate; listing missing items; locating value of missing items . . .
- Searching through boxes and boxes and paper bags filled with personal papers, to (hopefully) locate estate assets
- Cleaning, cleaning, cleaning, day after day after day
- Meeting with attorney
- Meeting with opposing family at opposing attorney's office
- Renting safe deposit box for estate
- Assessing which of Dad's assets could be liquidated to fund my executor duties
- Traveling to liquidate Dad's coin collection because we are unable to locate a local coin dealer

- Opening estate bank account with liquidated funds
- Turning on utilities under name of estate; challenging an outrageous water bill
- Meeting with attorney (many, many, many times more)
- Locating expert antique gun appraiser to provide appraisal on missing civil war rifle (a family heirloom) from photos taken by Dad
- Arranging to have filled dumpster removed and replaced
- Cleaning property day after day after endless day
- Arranging to have second, filled dumpster removed and replaced
- Spending hours on County Clerk website in an attempt to locate deed to property in another state
- Placing Dad's house on market
- Traveling to another state to locate mystery deed, possibly filed under an LLC (unable to locate deed)
- Holding yard sale because not enough items for estate sale; donating items that didn't sell
- Meeting with various local financial institutions to gather account information and beneficiary designations on accounts discovered to have been collected and closed by original executor
- Petitioning court for asset information from opposing family
- Signing over Grandmother's stock to "stepfamily"
- Hiring qualified CPA
- Applying for a Federal Employer Identification Number (FEIN) for the estate
- Paying taxes
- Writing estate summary

- Distributing remaining assets
- Petitioning court to close probate and relieve me of my duties

So much for "quickly and efficiently."

• • •

In the beginning of dreadful confusion, I sprinted onto the track as though we were in a race against the other estate. *After all, Dad's estate had already been in probate for over two years*, I reasoned. *Didn't we need to find his assets before the other side laid claim and the trail vanished?*

Turned out I could hurry all I wanted, but it wouldn't matter because the legal .... profession .... moves very .... very .... slow...............................ly.

• • •

Psst . . . don't tell anyone, but secrecy can be an estate plan's worst enemy.

Don't leave your executor in the dark! —As you can see, the responsibilities of an executor can be greatly underestimated. Had I lived in another state serving as a long-distance executor or worked a full-time job rather than as a stay-at-home mom, I wouldn't have had the ability or the time to handle everything that Dad's estate required. The amount of stress created by this particular situation would have been an impossible burden.

I cannot emphasize the importance of providing your executor with every bit of information they will need to efficiently fulfill their duties—*before* you enter that place of no return. Please don't keep them in the dark. Ignorance isn't bliss for the individual in charge of another's residual life without direction. And once you are gone, you won't be available for questions.

Before naming an executor, ASK your potential candidates AND their alternate(s) if they would be willing to serve. Explain what is expected and required of them. Bring everyone you name on board. Encourage team unity. It is just as crucial—if not more—for your alternate(s) to receive firsthand information as it is for your primary appointee. And in the process, your estate plan may receive some much-needed checks and balances.

Share all concerns about the potential behavior of "slighted" heirs or the disinherited. It is only right that everyone asked to serve is privy to your situation. Be honest about any dangers lurking in the background.

Discuss your assets, liabilities, and entire estate planning, with as much detail as feels comfortable. Allow candidates sufficient time to consider whether or not they are truly up to the task. And keep in mind that when the time comes, your nominee(s) can still refuse appointment or request to be released from their duties after appointment.

Consider your family's dynamics. Choose your executor accordingly. Recognize the mental and physical power they will possess, as well as any potential threats against them.

• • •

Senseless Tragedy—*In the news*: On December 15, 2004, a fifty-four-year-old man was arrested and charged with murdering his sister in the elementary school parking lot where she had just dropped off her six-year-old daughter. The man shot his sister eight times at close range by handgun.

At the time, police did not have a clear motive for the shooting but were aware of long-running family tensions. It seems two years prior, the brother had been specifically and officially disinherited by the siblings' father through his will.

The victim, however, was bequeathed and had been in control of the father's estate, all the while enduring threats and harassments from her unemployed brother, who had moved from Florida to Nevada to get "his fair share." According to court records, the estate was worth less than $200,000.

On March 13, 2008, the brother was sentenced to two consecutive life sentences without parole.

. . .

What appears to be extreme wealth may be nothing more than extreme indebtedness. Likewise, what some consider poverty might in truth be wealthy comfort.

Having been appointed executor without the benefit of a single piece of information, I was forced to do a blind search for assets. I began by consulting a financial advisor for direction. He concluded that because Dad had worked as a civil servant and had lived a frugal life, his estate probably consisted of nothing more than a modest checking account, savings account, and a life insurance policy of perhaps $5,000 or so. Throw in his house and car, I was told, and more than likely that was the sum of Dad's estate.

No one took into consideration the rest of the story. Dad had managed to avoid the three biggies of parenthood: braces, colleges, and weddings. Typical of his generation, he was a waste-not, buy-used-and-make-everything-else survivor of the Great Depression and Dust Bowl era. He had inherited a modest estate from his mother, including real estate and stock, which he had invested and let the proceeds grow untouched. He had invested in precious metals his entire life. Who would have known he had been a silent partner in a successful local business? As far as I knew, Dad was hardly the millionaire next door. But he was far more comfortable than the advisor assumed.

Either way, I shouldn't have been so clueless. From time to time, throughout the years, Dad would shove some paper or signature card in front of me and bark, "Sign here." I always signed without question. When my half-sister, Connie, and I got to know each other, she told me Dad had also instructed her to sign several mystery papers over the years. She had felt it would have been disrespectful to question his demands, and she was as clueless about what she had signed as I was. Each time I located an asset, along with its original signature card or beneficiary designation, it was surreal to discover our very own signatures from so long ago.

Dad believed secrecy and tight control protected his estate. Instead, thanks to secrecy, lack of communication, haphazard death-bed estate planning, and misleading attitudes about wealth, he created a hide-and-seek estate of frustration, where everything lost will never be found.

...

Hit the Pavement—The number of banking institutions in Dad's hometown were few enough that it was possible for me to visit each one, present my letters testamentary, and inquire as to whether or not Dad had been a customer. Originally, most of the customer service reps I spoke to told me they could do an in-house search for an hourly fee. Ultimately, I would learn the banks did not charge for account searches related to a customer's estate.

Making cold calls was humiliating. I was often viewed as suspect for not having adequate information. And although I was unaware in the beginning that Dad's accounts had already been closed and collected by Step-mum within one week to a month after Dad died—the banks knew. One bank refused to talk to me and asked me to leave. At another, a security guard followed me outside to write down my license plate number.

The untimely merging of banking institutions caused another obstacle to Dad's information. Those mergers created new staffs, changes in account numbers, and changes in protocol. In turn, the new account numbers created glitches in the staff's ability to retrieve closed-account information that "might or might not" have been programmed into the new computer systems.

Dad held accounts at four local banks and one that was out of state. I can't imagine having to search for missing assets with today's reliance upon online banking and paperless billing. I'm certain if the back window to Dad's house not been left open on that pivotal day, enabling me to gain access and to gather the receipts and information left behind, I wouldn't have found a single estate asset.

How would I have searched today without that paper trail? Now more than ever, thanks to online accounts, we must create, record, and share an open estate plan.

• • •

Contact the IRS—To request a copy of Dad's last filed tax return I used IRS Publication 559. The return would ultimately prove to be invaluable, providing the names of banking/financial institutions, brokerage firms, and some types of investment and business property. However, a tax return doesn't always reveal all assets, only those that reported interest, dividends or loss during that specific year.

I called the IRS for information and was directed to two or three different agents who were all very helpful. Because Dad and his wife had filed a joint return, I was first told that I would need permission from his wife's executor to request a copy of the return. Thankfully, it turned out that permission was not necessary.

• • •

Non-titled Property is the Wild West of probate, a no-man's land. That infamous spot where most schemes, betrayals, misunderstandings, and inheritance snafus are played out—just beyond range of the attorney's prying eyes. Well beyond a courtroom's reach.

Typically, an estate's attorney would never enter the trenches of an estate. Neither would the court. Their turf is limited to the endless piles of paperwork generated by the legal system. The attorney and the probate court may not be able, willing, or bound to protect and honor your instructions, especially concerning non-titled items.

And tomorrow, what shall tomorrow bring to the over-prudent dog burying bones in the trackless sand as he follows the pilgrims to the holy city?

KAHLIL GIBRAN, THE PROPHET

The Safe Deposit Box

Bingo! So this is where Dad's safe deposit box is.

I am waiting inside an office cubical at the third banking facility on my list. The lady who is helping me has left the room. After examining my notarized Letters Testamentary, she entered something into her computer, rose from her desk, and walked out the door. She hasn't confirmed anything yet, but I can tell. It's here.

At last I have managed to speak with authority, as though I am certain the box is at this location. Perhaps I feel more comfortable because this place is familiar, unlike the previous two banking facilities. Decades ago, Dad recommended that I open a savings account at this location. He even brought me here. *Now* I remember.

Several years ago, he added Connie's name to a checking account held at this institution for her use in an emergency. She still had a checkbook for the account and, for all she knew, could still write a check—if she were so inclined. She had never been informed otherwise.

"That's her." A heavy whispering from just beyond the doorway invades my thoughts.

"No! Tell her to leave."

I turn to catch a glimpse of an unidentifiable figure vanishing into the hallway. The lady returns but remains standing. She signals that our brief encounter has ended by slowly pushing her chair under her desk.

Then, with unflinching eye contact, she speaks. "I cannot tell you whether or not your father's safe deposit box is here. This is a federal institution. We do not recognize state-appointed personal representatives. That is all I can say."

Whoa, didn't see that coming! I am paralyzed. Quick. Think. What to do? Something strange is going on here. Very odd. Our eye contact turns to a glare. The lady is becoming agitated. She wants me to leave. Now.

Think. Think.

I open my notebook—the one every good executor should never leave home without—and prepare to write. "I want to get this straight," I state, "You are telling me that because this bank is a federal institution, you will not recognize my court-appointed authority over my father's estate?" I write. "And what is your name again? And your title?" There is a pause. Again, we make eye contact. She appears panicked.

Suddenly I am pawned off onto another lady from the front desk. But as I stand to leave the cubicle, I'm offered this non-confirmation: "I cannot say whether or not your father's safe deposit box is here. However, I can say that it is no longer open."

The lady from the front desk recommends an in-house search to find Dad's accounts, at a cost of $15 per hour, but, ironically, also refuses to recognize my authority. She informs me that I have no right to the information or to initiate a search. "Only those named on your father's accounts may request a search. "If," she adds, "they know the password."

It is Friday afternoon. We schedule a long-distance call between the branch manager and Connie for Monday morning at ten a.m.

On Monday Connie decides to go into work late to make the personal phone call without interruption. The effort is pointless.

Despite the fact that she is a joint tenant with right of survivorship on Dad's checking account, the manager refuses her request for a search. Connie does not remember the password. She is told that the personal representative (*Um, that would be me!*) will have to call to make the request.

Connie also learns that, as a joint tenant with right of survivorship, she could have withdrawn all of the money in the checking account upon Dad's death. However, it was a matter of who got there first. All but five dollars had been withdrawn by Step-mum seven days after Dad's death—over two years earlier. The account was still open with a five-dollar balance because the bank would have first required Connie's permission to close the account. (How thoughtful.)

The manager gave Connie the name of the next individual I would need to contact for assistance. I made an appointment. At last this runaround ended. An in-house search was authorized by my new contact, and contrary to what I had previously been told, the bank did not charge for information gathered for a client's estate.

• • •

Quite a Quandary—The 1933 gold "double eagle" is said to be the most valuable coin in the world. Why? Because none should exist. All 445,500 were supposed to have been melted down in 1934 rather than placed into circulation. A few, however, apparently flew the coop unscathed.

In 2003, ten of these rare birds were discovered inside the safe deposit box belonging to the deceased father of Joan Langbord.

What's an heir to do? Langbord entrusted the coins to the care of the Philadelphia Mint in order to confirm their authentication. Yep, they were real all right. Unfortunately, the mint refused to give them back, declaring the coins had to have been stolen from the Philadelphia Mint back in the 30s.

Langbord and her sons filed a lawsuit in US District Court in Philadelphia against the mint, the Treasury Department, and agency officials, in hope of retrieving the coins.

In 2011 a jury decided the coins still belonged to the government. The Langbord family appealed, and in 2015 was awarded rights to all ten coins, possibly worth $80 million, but celebration was short-lived. The government appealed, and a Federal court ruled in favor of the government.

The family next appealed to the United States Supreme Court. On April 17, 2017, the highest court in the land announced it would not hear the case. The coins remain in the custody of the government.

Keep the circus going inside you, keep it going, don't take anything too seriously, it'll all work out in the end.

DAVID NIVEN

Send in the Clowns

Two years into probate plus another five months into my appointment as personal representative, and after finding where the safe deposit box had been located, and after the strangers living in Dad's house moved off the property, a meeting was held. Stepmum's attorney, his assistant, two of the members from the opposing tribe, my attorney, and I gathered around a table too small for the occasion, cramped inside a meeting room on enemy territory. We passed a figurative peace pipe, from which none of us really inhaled, and spoke about some of the things that had happened, about the need for cooperation, and about wrapping up the mess.

The opposing attorney had preemptively advised his clients "to not fight over the magazine rack." So, the contents of Dad's safe deposit box, which apparently represented the magazine rack of his estate, was offered: two heavy boxes containing silver bars, coins, and bills, complete with an itemized inventory and list of estimated value (created by the opposing side). Everyone present agreed that I would liquidate this booty-turned-bounty to care for the estate—to get Dad's house fixed up, cleaned up, and ready for market.

It was also agreed upon that, once liquidated, the proceeds would be used to open an estate checking account. The situation was degrading, in that other people had control over our family matters and our family possessions. I didn't understand having to ask people I didn't even know—people who weren't even family—for permission. But I reminded myself to be thankful that the estate would at last be funded. *Hopefully, it would be enough to carry us through and there would be no more threat of out-of-pocket expenses.*

Our meeting ended in late afternoon, around rush hour, on a payday Friday before Halloween. Nervous about being responsible for the retrieved loot, I decided to secure it in a new safe deposit box at my bank on my way home.

The entire bank's staff was in costume. While a pleasant young man, dressed in 1920s' gangster garb, filled out the paperwork, I realized my dilemma. Exactly how would I carry those heavy boxes of silver and coins into the bank by myself? Multiple trips from the parking lot? Having to repeatedly check in and out of the safe area? Not to worry, reassured my new gangster friend. He would arrange for assistance. And yes, I could pull my car up to the front door.

Although customers occasionally parked at the spot out front in order to use the ATM, it felt wrong to pull up, park and open my trunk. It felt like I was taking part in some devious plan. A clockwork bank heist. But I followed my insider tip, and in a race against the bank's closing, pulled up, rushed out, opened my trunk, and turned to face a seemingly seven-foot-tall clown, complete in neon wig, accompanied by a shorter clown sidekick. *My assistants?*

I laughed. Perhaps, I laughed a bit more than was necessary because my assistants appeared perplexed. But how could they have known to appreciate the irony of the situation? That Dad's treasure was about to be carried back inside a bank and placed inside a safe by clowns. It was cosmic clown perfection.

A friend once told me that during a circus tragedy, the clowns are sent in to perform to divert the attention of the crowd. Tragedy and comedy. In circus as in life: *Send in the clowns.*

• • •

In the Bank—Two main duties of the executor are to conserve estate assets and not leave the assets stagnant. A separate account in the name of the estate and under its own Federal Employer Identification Number (FEIN) should be opened as soon as possible. All estate-related expenses are paid from this account. An interest-bearing account should also be opened as more cash assets are collected.

I opened a checking account in the name of Dad's estate with the liquidated contents of the safe deposit box. Bank employees mistakenly informed me that I could not use Dad's social security number for the estate account and that, after two years, an estate could no longer file for its own FEIN. I was told I would have to use my personal social security number.

Not comfortable with that idea, and not wanting to deal with the estate's interest mixing with my personal finances, I opened a non-interest-bearing checking account. Still, I was required to use my social security number. Three years later, the CPA hired to file the estate's return would inform me that not only could we still file for a FEIN, it was imperative we do so right away!

The public notice to creditors, notifying creditors of their right to file a claim against the estate, was placed in our local paper as required when the estate first opened. Therefore, the deadline for filing a claim had long passed since that time and was no longer relevant.

Note: Some states require creditors to be notified of the opening of the estate by letter.

Stock certificates are often stashed away and forgotten. In the meantime, companies move, merge, change names and dissolve. Tracing a company can be an extremely difficult task. Check the US Securities and Exchange Commission website for more information.

Dad never missed the nightly stock report, so I was well aware of his investment in stock. I found a few references to brokerage firms and gained another lead when a copy of his tax return arrived. Eventually, I found the actual statements to one of his brokerage accounts, but Dad had invested in stocks his entire life. Over the course of decades, he'd left a trail of firms and brokers across four states. I made inquiries at each local broker just as I had with the banks. I came up with a timeline of sorts from broker to broker to Step-mum's broker, but I'll never know if I found everything, especially out-of-state assets.

We located my grandmother's stock, but I had to sign the certificate over to "stepfamily." Let me tell you, that one broke my heart. But I was fortunate to be able to view such an aged, beautifully detailed certificate. They don't make 'em like that anymore. Keep in mind that a stock certificate with no cash value may still be worth something as a collectible.

The Search—Don't skimp on hiring a reputable title company to locate real property. At the time, many county clerk web sites provided tools for online title searches. Procedures varied throughout the country and, especially in the case of mystery property, the expertise of a trained title clerk is often necessary and in the case of Dad's estate, would have been well worth the cost.

Note: A separate probate called an ancillary administration must take place to transfer title to real property located in another state. An ancillary executor (usually an attorney in that state) will need to be hired to handle this administration.

Missing personal property? Good luck. We've all heard the horror stories about the relatives who "cleaned the house" while everyone else was still at the funeral service. Truth is, it's amazing what people will do and what people get away with.

Find out what means are available in your area to secure the property. Are you required to have a professional appraisal or estate audit? If an estate sale is necessary, hire a reputable estate liquidator. The unscrupulous often try to take advantage in this area as well.

Definition of a cynic: A man who knows the price of every-thing and the value of nothing.

OSCAR WILDE

Self-worth

We had received the "Affordable Life Insurance" offer countless, mindless times before, tucked inside our bank statements. Each month I would briefly consider the offer, only to toss it out of sight until the next statement arrived, déjà vu. Then one month, in a flash of what I mistook for an epiphany, I considered it, checked the rate, and made the call.

I told the agent that I wished to apply for a $150,000 life insurance policy.

"What type of work do you do?" the agent asked.
"I'm writing a book," I replied.
"How much money do you make?"
"Nothing at the moment."
"What type of work have you done in the past?"
"Nothing much, mostly been a homemaker."
"This is not a get-rich-quick scheme!" he barked. "The purpose of life insurance is to replace financial loss. *You* are not worth anything."
"I am in the process of settling my father's estate--"
"Ohh, I see," he injected. (Whatever "oh, I see" meant.)

"*And,*" I interrupted back, determined to make my case, "I want to make up for the inheritance my children stand to lose because, well–" (Wasn't a lost inheritance a financial loss?)

"How good of a writer are you?"

"I don't know," I replied timidly.

"Well, do you think you could make twenty-five thousand next year?"

"I don't know," I replied, sinking lower.

"Well, *maybe*, IF you can make twenty-five thousand next year, I *might* be able to insure you for twenty-five thousand. But that is, IF you are any good."

And this was how I discovered that my self has no worth.

"Self-worth" generated some interesting and telling remarks the night it was read to my writing group. One gentleman said my tale didn't make sense, and he was certain my details were wrong. "No one is denied life insurance. Change the life insurance in the story to disability insurance," he advised. "That would make sense."

"Why would the agent say that?" someone asked.

"Because she was not worth anything," stated another.

Not worth anything. In an instant, the men in our group seemed lost in thought. I imagined these words had sparked a male consensus of mental calculators clicking away: *Hmm, how much were the women in (and out of) their lives worth? What was their value?*

"I understand what she's saying," one lady offered. "This happened to me years ago when I applied for life insurance with my husband. I was a stay-at-home mom and the agent told my husband there was no reason to insure me because I had no income."

"Yes," someone else agreed. "Why would her husband need to buy a policy on her if she didn't make any money?"

From across my shoulder shot the quick-witted answer, "To pay for the next blonde."

I'm told my experience while attempting to apply for life insurance isn't a process normally guarded by snarling junkyard agents. So, I will assume the agent I happened upon that day had other issues on his mind—like calculating his own self-worth.

Two weeks after my group reading, an article appeared in our local paper about the monetary value of the stay-at-home mom. Turns out she is worth big bucks after all. But we already knew this—*right?*

As my attorney would later explain to me, the main purposes of life insurance are to: (1) provide those who depended upon you for financial support with the cash equivalent of what they would have received if you had not died; and (2) provide your estate with the amount of liquidity needed to cover estate-settling liabilities such as medical and funeral costs, creditor liens, legal fees, etc.

An adequate life insurance policy is the quickest, most efficient way to keep things rolling after you are gone. In most cases life insurance is tax-free and passes outside probate. However, certain arrangements can create exceptions. Consult your attorney, advisor, or agent for details.

The Elusive Life Insurance Policy—Often survivors are never told about a life insurance policy and therefore do not know they need to file a claim. Several leads to Dad's policies came from recorded entries found in checking account registries. Eventually, I also found a line-of-credit application listing the value of each policy, and a scrap of paper with a matching handwritten list of policies cashed in by Step-mum.

I consulted my personal, independent auto insurance agent for advice. He made a call regarding one of the potential policies and arranged a search. He also requested a photocopy of the canceled benefit check, which revealed the endorsement, banking institution, and account into which the check had been deposited over two years earlier. This was the only insurance company consulted that would provide assistance.

Other Sources to Consult:
- Previous employers
- Union or trade association
- Other groups in which testator was a member, such as alumni or auto club
- AARP membership
- Direct Selling Association
- Life insurance linked to a
    - * travel accident policy
    - * annuity
    - * pension, etc.
- Income tax return for life insurance interest received or paid on policy loans.

Other Uses of Life Insurance:
- Divorce agreement requires you to carry a specific amount
- Creates trust for dependent children
- Equalizes inheritances between beneficiaries

- Equalizes excessive support that was unintentionally provided to one child over another during your lifetime
- Provides a backup inheritance for children from previous marriage(s)
- Covers business ownership or co-ownership obligations
- **Creates an inheritance**
- **Covers child-care costs**
- **Pays college tuition(s)**
- Pays off mortgage and credit card debt
- Provides lifetime care for pet(s)
- Leaves money to non-heirs
- Leaves money to charity

Facts of Life:

- Basic coverage types: individual, or group (usually offered by employer)
- Basic policy types: term (expires) or whole (part insurance, part savings account, remains in force until you die)
- A general guide to the amount of life insurance needed is 5-10 times one's annual net salary
- An average funeral costs $8,500 (2018)
- An extra amount of life insurance is recommended to cover unexpected end-of-life expenses

Easily Overlooked—Month after month, a friend of mine struggled to rake together the extra $2,000 required for her terminally ill stepfather's care. It wasn't until after he passed away, while sorting through his personal papers, that she discovered he had owned a valid, untouched long-term care policy. *Oops!*

Unclaimed Property—Property usually becomes abandoned as a result of a change in name or address, or the owner dies and the heirs are unaware of the property or the heirs can't be located. Also, accounts are often forgotten or neglected (inactive) and, as a result, are declared abandoned.

Every state maintains an unclaimed property database, but unclaimed property laws vary. All companies, businesses and organizations are required to turn over abandoned property to the state's unclaimed property office. Most states will hold the property until claimed by its owner or heirs. After a prescribed amount of time, the contents of a safe deposit box may be auctioned off, but the proceeds will remain in trust until rightfully claimed.

Common Examples of Forgotten or Misdirected Property:

- Security deposits and refund checks
- Dividend checks from stock or mutual funds
- Safe deposit box contents
- Probate court judgments
- Life insurance benefits— (IF the company knows the owner has died and the beneficiary can't be located.)
- Long-term certificates of deposit, dormant checking and savings accounts
- Income tax refunds
- Royalty payments

Several "heir finder" scams have surfaced throughout the decades. Many scams have operated by mail or Email using bogus offers to help reunite the recipient with unclaimed money—for a fee, of course.

Although legitimate search firms do exist (a.k.a. locator, finder, tracer, heir finder, collector, investigator, researcher, broker, etc.) don't be fooled into paying for something you can do yourself with the click of your mouse free of charge.

If, for whatever reason, you decide to use a search firm, check that the firm is registered or licensed with your state. Also find out if your state places a limitation on finder fees. A finder fee is usually charged as a percentage of the total value of the recovered property—the cap may be set at ten to thirty percent. Be leery of locators who approach you and never, ever, pay a locator in advance! But seriously, there's no reason to hire anyone.

Otherwise, have some fun! Do searches for family and friends. Search for lost assets of long-lost relatives. Check every state lived in, worked in, and don't forget to check under former and maiden names. Each state provides instructions and forms necessary for filing a claim.

To date: The following sites are absolutely legit. On a whim, while checking these links in 2017, I searched Dad's name and found yet another, albeit teeny-tiny, unclaimed life insurance policy that belonged to my mother. And this was thirty-four years after she passed away and twenty years after Dad passed away! Lesson learned: keep on checking from time to time. You never know what might turn up.

- *National Association of Unclaimed Property Administrators (NAUPA): unclaimed.org*

- *Missing Money: missingmoney.com*

- A Consumer Alert on HUD.gov warns of "tracers" who offer to collect a HUD refund for a fee.

Wasted All Those Years

It is 2:20 a.m. For the fifth time tonight, I turn off the TV. I wish I could turn off my thoughts as easily.
JOURNAL ENTRY, SEPT. 1999

So many sleepless nights spent in worry trying to understand Dad's will. It was an intense, emotional time, filled with confusion and hostility knowing others—strangers—were in charge of our family things, including having to ask them for permission to sell my own father's home.

If only Dad had shared his instructions with my sister, Connie, and me in an open and direct manner. I am certain we wouldn't have faced a single problem. The transition would have gone as smoothly as Dad had envisioned 20 years earlier, and with the ease Grandmother had wished for the two of us—her only grandchildren. Dad's estate would have opened and closed a success.

Instead, the entire ordeal was suffocating. I was terrified by the situation, living each day—three years' worth of days—consumed by stress and fear. The less cooperation I received from the other side, the more I felt the need to document every single move I made, either in writing or by photo. I refused to go onto Dad's property without a witness. And although probate was unsupervised, I first asked my attorney for permission before doing anything and everything.

Looking back, I have to ask: what else might I have accomplished during all those years with all that wasted effort? What might I have accomplished instead with the energy and time spent—years lost—chasing after the wind?

Money is congealed energy.
JOSEPH CAMPBELL

Will Your Estate Be a Financial Burden?

The words "debt" and "expense" are not generally associated with "inheritance" or "beneficiary." But a mishandled estate, or an estate unprepared to deal with its own expense, can turn inheritance into debt and saddle its beneficiary or executor with needless financial burden.

Beginning with the funeral expense, the tab for settling an estate can quickly add up from payments to creditors, property management costs, and attorney fees. Pile on a troubled estate, and the tab increases by heaps and mounds. If the estate does not have accessible liquid assets to cover its expenditures, that tab could inadvertently fall upon those who are left behind.

It's also possible for a plan to focus too much on protecting "the money" from probate. By passing all liquid assets outside of the will directly to the beneficiaries (through use of joint ownerships and beneficiary designations), nothing may be left for the executor or trustee to cover initial expenses.

Monetary bequests are distributed *after* all estate expenses have been paid. If the estate's expenses slurped up every drop of liquid assets, other property may have to be sold in order to cover the monetary bequests.

Estate funds passed on to an individual through a joint ownership, or beneficiary designation, become the property of that individual. If such an arrangement was made and intended for estate use, but the recipient chose to keep the money instead, the recipient has a legitimate right to do so. Determine if it would be better to directly name the estate as beneficiary.

There are no hard rules to ensure an adequate, available supply of liquid funds for settling an estate or to fund a testamentary trust. Because each estate and each beneficiary situation are unique, so is the solution.

• • •

> *Say not that you know another entirely until you have divided an inheritance with him.*
>
> JOHN KASPER LAVATER (1784)

Heirs and Beneficiaries

The day Dad passed away I was certain I would never again have reason to return to his home. Who knew a couple of years later I would be back sorting through a mess, desperate for answers and searching for clues? Without that buffer of time, however, dealing with his estate would have been unbearable. It would have felt wrong to fight for anything or to stand up for anything, regardless of what I imagined Dad expected of me. It would have been necessary to simply let everything go.

From any angle, an inheritance is a complex, emotionally charged event involving a full range of real or imagined perceptions, from an heir's worth to a sterile sense of obligation to a validation of love. The inheritance may be received with guilt, accepted with profound gratitude or seized with eager anticipation. But heirs who are forced to fight for their inheritance have a difficult time finding comfort.

Somewhere within a verbal grocery list and talking about dry cleaning, my mother announced that my "father's daughter" would be coming for a visit. Just like that, I learned of Connie's existence from a previous marriage.

I was twenty-three. Connie was thirty-six.

Our father's tendency toward keeping his personal relationships separated kept Connie and me apart for most of our lives. It was his final illness, death and the resulting probate process that ultimately brought us together as sisters and as friends.

Without that newly found connection and source of endless support, I could not have survived the bizarre ordeal with my sanity intact. With each crisis, large or small, Connie was available by phone for everything, from words of encouragement to mutual venting sessions. There was little that we did not agree upon. But as crisis upon crisis turned months into years, my unrelenting phone calls and the great distance between us became increasingly frustrating for her.

The following is Connie's perspective as a long-distance heir to a chaotic estate among strangers:

As Dad's condition worsened, *I relied on Ann for information and I think she relied on me as the voice of reason in the dying process. At one point Ann was told Dad had sleep apnea, and she was instructed to monitor his breathing. She was also warned Dad did not have a Do Not Resuscitate Order (DNR) and was told if he did stop breathing, she would be obliged to perform CPR. When Ann called me with such ridiculous statements, I hope I was able to bring some reason back to what was happening and that I gave her at least a small amount of support.*

When Dad died, it was Ann's daughter, Shelley, who tried to contact me. My new relationship with Ann settled a pressing problem I had discussed with my sister, Debbie, when it became obvious Dad was not going to get better: Where would I stay when I had to go to the funeral? I had decided on a hotel, but Ann invited me to stay with her. Being in her home helped give me the support I needed at the time and a chance to meet her husband, Leo.

When the funeral was over, I left for the airport and my life in New Orleans. Ann and I promised to stay in touch and visit each other in the future. At the time we didn't have any idea how much in touch we would stay and what my future visit would entail. Neither of us thought in terms of a will or Dad's wishes about his belongings and financial state. We had just lost our father—our foremost thought—no matter what our relationships had been with him.

I think several years went by. At least that is what it seemed like. Ann and I kept in touch as we had resolved, but one day out of the blue the can of worms opened. Ann received a phone call informing her that Dad's wife had passed away. We hadn't known anything about Dad's will until someone Ann knew overheard someone else talking about it.

Thanks to that coincidence, we soon realized probate on Dad's estate had not been closed and Ann should take over as executor. Thus, began the long and arduous task Ann describes in this book. My role in the process consisted mostly of talking to Ann by phone and, as the years went by, trying to understand what in the hell Dad was thinking of.

We all knew Dad to be painfully honest. He would have cut a penny in fourths to make things equal. But what he left us was a mess, and we had to live with the mess he had given us. Ann had to live with more of a mess than I did. My role was supportive. She would call me, and we would talk about troubles. We had to come to terms with our losses and eventually we did just that.

All the while, Ann was busy cleaning Dad's house and getting it ready for sale. During the process, she was the most tenacious person I have ever been acquainted with. Ann was determined to know about Dad's possessions and what had happened to each and every thing. Suffice it to say that she astounded me with every phone call and the information she came up with. She pieced together Dad's estate, and she had a detailed record of what she had found.

The following years were filled with phone calls, sometimes as many as three or four a week. Her frustrations came from having to call and reverse something she had just told me a few days before. Mine came from being so far away and from not being able to follow everything she told me.

I would find myself struggling to remember our last conversation. Ann had all of the facts well chronicled in her head and on paper. I did not. I would end up just telling her to do what she felt was best and easiest for her to do. I do believe Ann was put in as the third executor just for show. But one thing I came to understand very well over time, if my name had been put in as executor, I would have had an agent sell the house and I would have let everything else get away.

Dawn and Dusk

By Roy E. Perry

At early morn, with stars
still twinkling in the sky,
We walk along, my hand in his,
Granddad and I, out to the pond.
The day is still-aborning.
No warmer glow than
Lanterns in the morning.

At twilight time, with fireflies
dancing in the sky,
We walk along, his hand in mine,
Grandson and I, down to the creek.
The night beyond conceiving.
No sweeter smell than
Lilacs in the evening.

Forgotten: A Granddaughter's Sorrow

My Oklahoma grandpa resides in the imagination of the great-grandchildren he never knew through endearing tales of loving guidance. In contrast, the lack of memories my children hold of their own maternal grandfather will forever remain a heavy settling of disappointment.

The following is authored by my daughter, Shelley, as she provides an honest view of the impact felt by a grandchild who is ignored, forgotten—and through a bizarre twist of events—ultimately replaced.

The day my grandfather died I was right there by the hospital bed, which was positioned in the middle of his living room. My father had just called to tell me he was on his way over to pick me up and take me home. He told me to say goodbye to Grandpa as though this would be the last time I would see him.

I walked into the living room and looked at Grandpa. I was fifteen, and this was the first time I had been near death. I had absolutely no idea what to say. I just stared at the man I had thought would live forever—the man who was tall and noble-like. The man who wore khaki pants with a nicely pressed button-down white shirt always tucked into a small black belt.

At that moment I was looking at only the shell of that man. He wasn't my grandfather and, even if he were, how do you say goodbye to a man you hardly knew—a man who didn't invite you to know him?

One of the earliest memories I have of my grandfather is when I was around seven or eight years old. He knocked on our front door and, without stepping inside, he motioned for me to follow him to the trunk of his car. As I stood next to him, I watched him open the trunk and pull on white gloves. He reached in and handed me a plastic bag filled with empty soda cans that were freshly washed and dried. I thanked him and watched him remove his white gloves, get into his car and drive away.

I have many memories like that. Looking back on the actual day he died I wonder what he would have thought about the situation. He was an obsessive-compulsive, lying on a bed in his living room in a hospital nightgown, with no white gloves in sight.

The day he died I was still thinking of different things to say to him, not yet speaking them out loud, when he started to breathe oddly. Everyone rushed into the room. Grandpa's wife and her daughter stood on his left side, which is where I followed. My mother and father came in on my right with me, ironically, being the dividing line in between. The left side was trying to call him back and the right was quietly letting him go. I stood there watching, never saying goodbye. And who would have thought that situations prior to Grandpa's death would set the course of our lives for many years ahead?

After my mother dealt with my grandfather's estate for a length of time, it seemed like it was finally coming to a close. One of the many things needed to be wrapped up was the distribution of his property and estate to his heirs, according to his so-called will.

Whenever I accompanied my mom to the lawyer's office, the topic of grandkids would always come up. In the beginning, I chalked it up to being in my teens and not listening properly. I thought "everyone" meant my brother and me. The "grandkids" who were referred to were four kids who had absolutely no relation to us or my grandfather. It took me many years later to somewhat understand the reasoning how those kids ended up replacing us. I remember the day it finally sank into *my teenage mind that I wasn't considered the "grandkid." My brother and I weren't even considered at that time.*

All I could think of was, "I am the grandkid!"

. . .

What memories will you leave behind to family and friends? Have you taken the time to stop and express a personal validation to each loved one rather than assuming each one knows how you feel?

Are the memories you hold of a particular loved one stuck inside a trench of disappointment? Could it be the loved one was simply unaware of the need—or unable—to express sentiment?

What Does Your Estate Plan Really Say?

How many hopes and fears, how many ardent wishes and anxious apprehensions are twisted together in the threads that connect the parent with the child?
SAMUEL JOHNSON

Begin with an adult child's lifelong struggle to attain validation from the father: The Brass Ring. Add an emotionally detached father with tunnel vision about preserving his hard-earned money (the family wealth.) Toss in an estate-planning attorney intent on safeguarding the father's money from every imagined dragon of abuse for generations to come and, voila! The child is doomed to inherit a cauldron of disappointment.

Estate planners design plans with the heir in mind. But their emphasis will often rest upon "how best to protect the assets" *from* the heir for sake of the heir, and for the sake of future investment.

Examples of this focus are found in estate planning books that offer scenarios and advice on how to protect a child's inheritance from all types of hypothetical demons, including creditors and medical debt. I say, lighten up. So what if your son uses his inheritance to pay off creditors? Paying off creditors can be life altering in huge, positive ways. So what if your daughter uses her inheritance to pay for medical expenses? Why deny her the opportunity to heal with peace and security? Would you prefer she remain sick and stressed under the relentless pressure of bill collectors? To have money for medical insurance, let alone to cover the cost of expenses, can be life changing as well—literally.

What message do you extend to your adult child when you not only leave him a trust that is controlled by a sibling or a stranger, but termination of the trust requires the child to first pass a psychiatric evaluation? By attempting *to protect your money* from every conceivable situation or thing that *might* come up in the future lives of your heirs, your priorities become skewed. The estate does become about the money, not the people.

Before finalizing your estate plan, imagine yourself as each beneficiary. Take a reflective look at the final messages your plan extends. Does it say:

I don't trust you.

You aren't worth as much.

You are incompetent.

I'll never believe in you.

Is your plan a death-grip attempt at controlling the lives of those you failed to control while you were living? Have you offered this bequest with a joyous heart—or relinquished your possessions begrudgingly? Have you provided solace—or pitted family against one another?

Think about it. A will is the final communication by the deceased directed toward the living. This means the one who is gone gets to have the last say, the last laugh, the last *How do you like them apples*? Or it can be the last *I love you.*

The one who is gone has the power to pass down a final, irrevocable, one-sided, nonnegotiable judgment upon the living. Or to extend a priceless gift of eternal validation. Once you are gone, there are no takebacks. Proceed with caution because nothing cuts deeper than the final insult from the grave.

When Esau heard his father's words, he burst out with a loud and bitter cry and said to his father, "Bless me—me too, my father.

But he said, "Your brother came deceitfully and took your blessing."

Esau said, "Isn't he rightly named Jacob? He has deceived me these two times: He took my birthright, and now he's taken my blessing!" Then he asked, "Haven't you reserved any blessing for me?"

GENESIS *27:34-36*

I'll Be Dissin' You, Always

I've had the vantage of both sides: I believed my sister, my family, and I were technically disinherited by Dad; then I discovered his estate had been mishandled, abused, and after the passing of his third wife, it fell upon me to straighten out his affairs. Surprisingly, in retrospect, I much prefer the disinherited side. There is certain finality to it, despite the outcome, which cannot be found in a poorly planned, poorly articulated, and poorly administered estate.

Most will challenges are made by family members who believe they have been unjustly excluded from an estate because estate plans were never openly and honestly explained. You may feel you do not owe your children an inheritance, but you do owe them an explanation.

Be specific about who you plan to disinherit and state why, especially if this individual would naturally assume to be your heir. If possible, explain your decision to this individual, and to everyone who will be involved in your estate, *before* you are gone.

If you would prefer to have an individual learn of his or her disinheritance through your will after you are gone, specify the name of the disinherited directly in the will document and, without being offensive, provide a clear explanation. Remember, a probated will is a public document. Avoid unnecessary disclosure and undue tackiness. Never use your will to shame, punish, or judge.

To simply omit the disinherited from your will by not mentioning them at all might be the easiest way out now, but do you really want to take a chance on creating a hell on earth for everyone left behind? Do you really hate your disinherited heir so much that your goal is to torture them with eternal silence and confusion?

In order to make a major change, such as disinheritance, a new will should be created to replace the existing will. Never mark notations, corrections, or amendments on the original will document. To mark directly upon a will may negate its validity and doing so risks creating a situation of an unintentional disinheritance.

Before amending or revoking your current will, gather up the original and all copies. Immediately after the replacement document is properly created and signed, destroy the old original and all copies.

To avoid an accidental disinheritance, update your will after every major life event such as divorce, marriage, birth, adoption, and the selling or giving away of a major asset. Simple amendments to a will may be made through a codicil, rather than by replacing the entire will. However, a codicil should not be used to change beneficiaries or to disinherit.

Never disinherit or make changes to your estate plan in anger. Avoid pitting heirs against one another. Provide a clear explanation for significant inheritance inconsistencies among your children. Again, it would be ideal to discuss reasons with your heirs before you are gone.

Willed distributions are not written in stone and voluntary adjustments to equalize inheritances may be initiated by your beneficiaries. For example: a beneficiary who is willed an extra-large piece of estate pie may voluntarily refuse that particular slice and, to maintain family harmony, request a serving equal to the others. Or, as a group, beneficiaries might request an inheritance adjustment creating equal distribution for all. Also, for whatever reason, a beneficiary might choose a self-imposed disinheritance by altogether refusing his or her inheritance or refuse to accept joint survivorship assets.

In order to make such adjustments, the beneficiary would be required to sign a *disclaimer*. Generally, this document must be executed within nine months of death. Additional rules apply.

It may be nearly impossible to disinherit a legal spouse. State laws vary here. If you plan to disinherit or to leave an exceptionally small amount of your estate to your spouse, ask your attorney about a spouse's right to "elect against a will." Also, hiding assets in attempt to keep them from your spouse is never a solution.

Currently, Louisiana is the only state that prohibits disinheriting children.

Reminder: When a will is declared invalid and there is no valid will to replace it, as far as the court is concerned, you have died intestate—meaning, without a will. The court will then identify your legal heirs and distribute your estate according to state intestate law. Ask yourself: Is disinheriting really necessary? Would it place unnecessary hurt upon the disinherited or harm upon others?

• • •

Goodbye, Trouble—*In the news*: When hotel billionaire Leona Helmsley died, she left behind a $10 million inheritance to each of two grandchildren, she disinherited two other grandchildren, and she left a $12 million trust fund to her dog, a white female Maltese named Trouble. She also left specific instructions in her will that Trouble should be buried next to her in the Helmsley mausoleum.

However, even the mega-rich can't have everything they wish. Turned out her request won't be honored because, according to the New York Department of State's Division of Cemeteries, it is illegal for a dog to be buried in a cemetery meant for humans.

Update: In 2008, a judge found Leona mentally unfit at the time her will was executed, reduced Trouble's inheritance from $12 million to $2 million, awarded $4 million to the Helmsley Charitable Trust, and the remaining $6 million to the two grandchildren who had been disinherited through her will.

Trouble passed away December 13, 2011, at the doggie age of around sixty-four. According to a *New York Times* article, she was cremated and her remains "privately retained." The article also notes that since Ms. Helmsley is buried in a mausoleum, which is considered private property, and it wouldn't be impossible for someone with a key to let Trouble in.

Let there be no sadness at my funeral.
God has given me a life of usefulness,
a thousand friends, and a million blessings,
and I leave this world with a heart full of praise
and gratitude.

WORDS LEFT BEHIND BY MY GRANDMOTHER,
READ BY THE MINISTER AT HER FUNERAL SERVICE.

I heard this for the first time on a cassette tape discovered inside a dusty box of family photos recovered from Dad's garage.

And there are those who give and know not pain in giving, nor do they seek joy, nor give with mindfulness of virtue;

They give as in yonder valley the myrtle breathes its fragrance into space."

Through the hands of such as these God speaks, and from behind their eyes He smiles upon the earth.

KAHLIL GIBRAN, THE PROPHET

A Hug from Mabel

Anyone seeking a friendly helping of homegrown conversational wisdom could always find a welcoming spot at Mabel's kitchen table. Fittingly, it was during a series of kitchen-table conversations, garnished by a unique blend of humor and uninhibited candor, that Mabel and her daughter planned for the inevitable. Little by little, her final wishes were recorded on a plain piece of paper stored inside the family Bible. And when the time came, her simple riches were lovingly distributed in the spirit intended—absent of secrecy or pretense, full of grace. A reflection of Mabel's life.

Mabel was my neighbor, my friend, my surrogate mom. In life, she taught me what it meant to love without judging and to give without effort. With the endowment of her winter jacket—my hug from Mabel—she taught me how love can affirmatively transcend death and time through the simplest of gestures.

Whether an estate is considered large or small, the significance of our final communications will be forever emphasized in the minds of our heirs through the objects we bequeath.

The ethical will stems from a tradition dating back to

medieval times. Usually written in letter form, it is a nonlegal, loving bequest of one's life experiences and values. The ethical will is also used to provide personalized instruction and meaningful insight regarding the material bequests made through one's traditional will.

Devoid of clarification, a will can easily become a document of family ruin. Yet it is not the will itself that creates contentions within a family, and discord does not simply materialize upon inheritance of the family wealth. A will is merely a platform upon which the drama of all pre-existing issues might be spotlighted onto center stage and solidified into one-sided permanence.

Word

Believe it or not, your will doesn't need to be written in confusing legal jargon. The simpler the language, the better. However, the wording used does need to be direct and your instructions clear.

- Identify each beneficiary, in each instance, by full name. Do not simply use grandson, cousin, daughter, etc.
- Be cautious when using the words beneficiary and heir. Technically, a beneficiary is an individual named in a will to receive a bequest. An heir is an individual identified according to state intestate law if you were to die without a will.
- Identify property in detail. Don't say, "I give my car . . ."—provide the make, year, model, plate number, etc. Don't say, "I give my land . . ."—identify the land by parcel number and description.
- Understand the meaning of any legal term used,

such as per stirpes, per capita, and issue. If misused, these tiny words can have a huge impact upon the distribution of your estate. (As a matter of fact, check that you understand the implications of all words and terms used, simple or not.)
- Avoid oversimplified will instructions such as, "I leave my estate to my children 50/50"; or "I leave my residual estate to . . ."; or "I place all my assets in trust . . ." Define (with-in reason) what is residual. List and specifically identify all assets to be placed in trust.
- Remember, just because you said so in your will, doesn't mean it can be done. For example, you cannot change the name of a beneficiary to your life insurance policy through your will. Be certain that your instructions—and terminology—are correct, legal, and valid in your state.
- Attorneys can be wrong. Check that the two of you are on the same page.
- What wasn't said often causes more damage than what was said.
- Sentiment and use of endearments are good things.
- Leave out all words that are vague. For example: instead of saying, "I wish to leave my . . ."—say, "I give my . . ."

. . .

Precatory: Expressing a wish or desire but not creating a legal obligation or affirmative duty. Note: When interpreting wills, courts look to

> *whether a direction is precatory or mandatory in carrying out the testator's intent. Thus, courts generally will not construe language to create a trust if the language is only precatory and there is no evidence that the language was intended to create a trust. Words such as "with the hope that" or "it is my wish that" are often considered precatory.*
>
> MERRIAM-WEBSTER'S DICTIONARY OF LAW.
> 1996 MERRIAM-WEBSTER, INC.

• • •

Say What?—There is no shame in asking your attorney to define the meaning of any word, term, or law. After all, this is (we hope) his area of expertise, not yours. Be certain there are no assumptions and misunderstandings and that your attorney has provided you with clear explanations. Bottom line: Leave absolutely no room for interpretation!

• • •

If you find it too difficult to express sentiment in written form, as many of us do, don't feel disheartened. A trusted friend or family member might be willing to stand in as your own Cyrano de Bergerac. Or search ethical will websites for letter examples, to locate professional assistance, or to order various guidebooks. Again, use caution.

Self-expression needn't be limited to letter form,

however. For example, when my kids were young, I worried something might happen to me before I had the opportunity to pass on my "wisdom." So I gathered together my favorite poems, quotes, and music lyrics, which I felt summed up the things I wanted them to know about life, and copied these into one personalized journal for each child.

Check out the selection of theme books or figurines of various sentiments available at your local book or gift stores. Or how about dedicating a personal song to each loved one?

If you are the least bit creative, scrapbooking or a picture slide show set to music and recorded onto DVD can express your sentiments. A memory box filled with ticket stubs to events attended with the grandkids or filled with their artwork, letters, and cards you have saved is an easy, loving validation. You might keep a journal, or perhaps you would be more comfortable expressing yourself through a video recording to provide a casual, affirming chat with friends and loved ones.

The possibilities are endless.

Your message—priceless.

If thou art rich, thou'rt poor,
For like an ass, whose back with Ingots bows,
Thou bear'st thy heavy riches but a journey,
And death unloads thee.

S<small>HAKESPEARE</small>, M<small>EASURE FOR</small> M<small>EASURE</small>

. . .

A ruin is more than a collection of debris. It is a place with its own individuality, charged with its own emotion and atmosphere and drama, of grandeur, of nobility, or of charm. These qualities must be preserved as carefully as the broken stones which are their physical embodiment.

C<small>HRISTOPHER</small> W<small>OODWARD</small>, I<small>N</small> R<small>UINS</small>

Ransacked

All that remained had been tossed aside, creating mounds of things broken or unwanted. Estate rubble. A mockery. We build and collect and store and admire. In an instant, it is gone, like desert sand in the wind.

Who took what and when? What had been given away or sold? I would never know the truth. I could only know what was left. A court order had allowed me and an assistant onto Dad's property to take inventory.

As we stood inside the garage, knee-deep in chaos after having surveyed the disarray on the grounds and inside the house, as well, we decided we should return with a video camera. Making a list would not be possible.

After that day, anyone who saw the situation firsthand, advised me to bring in a loader, scoop everything up, and bury it. "Don't even bother sorting through," they said. It was a tempting proposition. The problem was I still didn't know what belonged to Dad's estate. And how could I not sort through? Concealed within these hallowed heaps, displaced and trashed, was the residue of my ancestry. Family history ended here.

Mr. Showmanship

> *I dedicate this book to all of you who believe in the true meaning of love; love that is shared and not possessed but cared for like a precious treasure that cannot be replaced.*
>
> LIBERACE, THE THINGS I LOVE

The Liberace Museum and Foundation was once located at 1775 E. Tropicana Avenue, Las Vegas, and featured "Dazzling Jewelry, Cars, Costumes: in Trust," from the personal collection of the most flamboyant man the world had ever seen.

Born Wladzin Valentino Liberace, hailing from Wisconsin, Liberace was one of television's earliest and most successful entertainment icons. With engagements in Las Vegas and throughout the globe, Liberace netted an income allowing him to acquire extravagances covering just about anything—literally. From jewelry to costumes to pianos to cars, the man covered a whole lot of things with rhinestone-and-etched-mirror-tile bling.

Wandering through the museum, a visitor couldn't help but be amazed by the outlandish display of materialism gone wild. Looking closer, beneath all of the sparkle and show, one would discover the unique reverence Liberace held toward the material wealth that had been "placed in [his] care." In Liberace's eyes, no object could ever lose its luster.

This touching perspective is also revealed in his autobiography, *The Things I Love*, which begins:

> *I Would Like to Be Remembered . . . as a kind and gentle soul, and as someone who made the world a little better place to live in because I had lived in it. Obviously, I would like to think*

> that my music will be remembered. But I hope also that some of the beautiful things I have collected in my homes will be preserved . . .
>
> I feel that all these beautiful things I live with have been placed in my care to look after. They don't really belong to me; they belong to the world. After all, they belonged to famous people before me—somewhere, somehow, they had been abandoned or not cared for. Then I came along and saw a broken chair or an unwanted dog or a forgotten antique that cried out to be saved . . . I find there is a great tendency, especially in our country, to tear out the old and build up the new—with no regard for tradition or the relics of the past.

The Liberace Foundation for the Performing Arts has awarded over $6 million in scholarships to students, colleges, and universities since 1976.

> For current locations, events, and information, go to: liberace.org.

The Power Within

> *The obvious often might be invisible because the more common an object, the more familiar an object, the less noticeable it becomes.*
>
> LOBSANG RAMPA, THE SAFFRON ROBE

Before we realize what has happened, time transforms the everyday into the subliminal: our possessions; the things we pass by on our way to work; the things in our office; even people in our lives simply fade away, day by day, before our eyes. It is here, transformed into an existence beneath our threshold of consciousness, where the smallest possession can evoke the greatest comfort—or wreak the greatest harm.

Objects associated with experiences of joy and with people we love radiate feelings of security and happiness. These might be Grandfather's hat, Mom's cookbook, a certain blanket from home. In contrast, some objects embody times of trauma, loss, anger, disappointment, and insult—all that is negative.

Possessions that conjure powerful and sentimental, yet conscious, connections with times gone by—such as a flower pressed between the pages of a book, a bundle of cards placed inside a trunk, a partially burnt candle kept in a drawer, a photo album—are typically tucked away and lie dormant until reawakened by our touch.

"Happy Happies" were what Liberace called "things that make people smile." Which of your possessions make you happy? Is it possible that one (or more) has a negative impact upon your environment by affecting your daily mood without you being aware? Does it perhaps even cause illness? Are feelings of anger or other negative memories sparked without explanation each time upon entering a particular room? Or do you experience peace throughout your space?

Take an emotional-attachment inventory of the objects in your home, car, and personal spaces. Discover and remove items attached to negative feelings and unpleasant events. Acknowledge and place the positive things within plain (subliminal) sight.

Talk to your heirs about which family items hold special or negative meaning for them.

...

When her grandfather died, my friend was the first in line to seek her inheritance: "I want Pawpaw's hat."

Luckily, no one argued.

The hat was well-worn and not the cleanest or the best-looking hat around, but in my friend's eyes, it was as priceless as a jeweled crown.

"Pawpaw always wore this hat," she explained to me while lovingly storing it away. "This hat *is* Pawpaw."

I've thought about the meaning of that old hat many times over the years: how the love held within such a simple possession was reflected on my friend's face that day. I hope it wasn't left inside that trunk but that it was brought out and hung on the hat rack by the door or on the back of a kitchen chair. I hope my friend indulged in its unassuming gift of everyday joy, because it could never hold the same power for anyone else.

And the Ties That Bind

> *Mary adds, "It was my grandfather's song, and he passed it to my mother, Pansy Hudson, an Elder, told me that I was to have the family song after Mom died."*
>
> STEVE WALL AND HARVEY ARDEN, WISDOMKEEPERS:
> MEETINGS WITH NATIVE AMERICAN SPIRITUAL ELDERS

Envision an estate so basic where all that remains of one's life is a song.

A funeral ritual of the Native American Hoh tribe, as described in the beautiful book, *Wisdomkeepers*, is to burn all of the personal belongings of the deceased "so that there is nothing to hold the one who has passed away to this world." To implement the ceremonious post-death burning of one's personal belongings in our material girl world is a tad unrealistic. Not to mention wasteful and dangerous. Talk about eternal flames! But the concept of this rite—to free the soul from all earthly attachments—offers something to consider.

What chains have you placed upon your life?

Take an internal inventory. Evaluate your balance sheet. Have you lived a life bound to the things you own and the things you believe you *must* own? Are you bound to irrational desires? Are you weighted down by what is intangible and unseen, yet is the heaviest of mortal burdens: grudges, hatred, revenge, disappointment, or even love?

What life issues need resolution? What relationships need mending? If you died today, would your soul be released into peace? Or entangled by regret?

What is your family song? What is your life song? Have you danced?

. . .

The emotional, physical, financial, and time-consuming burden of tending an estate, compounded by the amount of possessions owned today, makes itemized estate appraising a difficult task. Items that have always been around, passed down through the generations, risk becoming lost to the chaos or taken for granted by family, so the monetary value is never realized.

In 2006, a 1923 watercolor, anonymously dropped off at Goodwill, sold for $165,000 during the organization's online auction. Obviously, it was not known whether or not the mystery donor had been aware of the painting's worth. But I can imagine a family member who "always hated that ugly, old painting," eagerly letting go without considering its true value.

Don't neglect to share insider information and helpful guidance regarding the liquidation of any valuable possession or collection. Let your beneficiaries and your executor know who can be contacted and trusted to provide an honest appraisal. Include itemized lists and estimated values, a list of trusted buyers and sellers, and a list of anyone whom you would *not* trust to do business with. Most importantly, give a heads up on any potential scams. After all, you have had a great deal of time to learn about such details, but your executor/beneficiaries might not have the luxury of time to educate themselves.

Precious and Princess

Roy E. Perry

Precious and Princess were canine companions
Of Abigail Wentworth in Rome.
She offered them dainties, and called them her angels
And pampered them both in her home.

But Princess and Precious were never as saintly,
As the sweet little lady supposed.
Spoiled, rotten, and yappy, and both holy terrors,
They did what good breeding opposed.

Their names were misnomers, for Precious and Princess
Were lacking in manners and grace.
They'd snarl and they'd growl, they'd bark and they'd howl,
At all who dared enter their space.

When Abigail Wentworth went to her long rest,
Within her freshly dug grave,
Princess and Precious grieved at her passing,
And tried their best to be brave.

They whined and they whimpered when Parsifal took them
(Miss Abigail Wentworth's chauffeur)
And drove them way out to the sticks and the boonies,
And threw them both from the car.

Displaced Loyalty

Our most trusted companions are not merely things we possess. They are living, breathing, thinking, and, yes, *reasoning* beings. They stand by us, protect us, comfort us, depend upon us, and love us—no matter what.

And they grieve when we are gone.

They are creatures of habit (aren't we all?), finding comfort in the routines we have arranged for their daily lives. Like children, they are extensions of our personalities, yet unique in their own right. We become their life. They become our responsibility.

Until a few years ago, I was not aware that pets are sometimes euthanized upon the death of their owners. I was horrified by this revelation. How could anyone allow this to happen in today's society? Then again, how many have taken the time to create a legitimate plan of care, should our pets outlive us?

Create a pet journal to inform a future caretaker about your pet's vaccines, routines, habits, preferences, and quirks. Record any known illness and any behavioral warning signs you have observed in your pet that would precede an episode of illness. The more difficult the pet, the more important it is to provide honest insight into its behavior and needs.

In 2004 I adopted a five-year-old cat named Bailey through a local shelter. Basically, she was a very good girl and a great companion. But a few issues came to light over the years, which a caretaker with no patience might not have been willing to deal with.

My son flat-out told me, "I hate your cat." Bailey's feelings were mutual toward his entire family, which at the time included a toddler, a pre-teen, and their own cat, Lilly. You see, Bailey was never good with children, and she never got along with other animals.

Obviously, my son was not nominated as a caregiver.

Update: Bailey peacefully crossed over the rainbow bridge, at the age of nineteen, while at home on her sofa, and under the care of a mobile pet hospice.

"Now there were seven brothers. The first one married and died without leaving any children for his brothers. The second one married the widow, but he also died, leaving no child. It was the same with the third. In fact, none of the seven left any children. Last of all, the woman died too. At the resurrection, whose wife will she be, since the seven were married to her?"

Jesus replied, "Are you not in error because you do not know the Scriptures or the power of God? When the dead rise, they will neither marry nor be given in marriage; they will be like the angels in heaven."

Mark 12:20-25

Grave Decisions

Mom and Dad had been married thirty-seven years when Mom passed away. Her place of rest is a plot in a quaint cemetery tucked away down an Oklahoma country road near her birth-place—a once-upon-a-town named "Goodnight." They had chosen and purchased the side-by-side double plot and double headstone decades before Dad died. It was a given that Dad would spend eternity right there next to Mom—until his last wife made other arrangements.

After Dad passed away, I learned he would not be sent back to Oklahoma for burial and back to Mom. I wasn't even certain Mom would still want him, under the circumstances. What I hadn't realized until too late, however, was how Dad's wife had plotted (pun intended).

For weeks after Dad's burial, my daughter and I kept a graveyard watch, waiting for his headstone to appear. In the meantime, we talked about what type of stone we would have ordered and what it would say.

Shelley spotted it first. Dad had a headstone all right. So did his wife, her headstone placed precisely above his. In other words, when her time came, Dad's last wife was to be buried, not alongside, but *on top of* Dad!

My parents had never talked about visiting or tending gravesites. If they worried about such things, they did so in secret. Besides, all of our deceased family members resided in cemeteries two states away. Dropping by for a graveside chat or for seasonal decorating was not a convenient option. Through our family's non-tradition I learned that, unlike our physical self, the soul doesn't require a permanent address, and free spirits can be conjured up for good conversation from any spot, at any time. At least in one's imagination.

But after Dad's passing, I found that unresolved issues between the living and the dead are another matter entirely. They seem to require a tangible spot to be properly aired and exorcised of any determined demons—a tangible and private spot with no one in between.

Thanks to Step-mum's eternal presence, no one in our family has since, or ever will, visit Dad's grave.

The double headstone and empty plot next to Mom in Oklahoma felt like sad, unfinished business. Yet it hadn't occurred to me that anything could be done until I mentioned the situation to my attorney. He told me I could arrange to have the headstone replaced. That was the very first thing I took care of after discovering and recovering funds from a misdirected joint account, which had been in Dad's and my name.

I worried I would have a difficult time locating the caregivers because the cemetery in Oklahoma is cared for by volunteers. But everything went along as easy as country pie. Everyone I spoke with was accommodating, caring, and eager to help. I ordered a new, single headstone decorated with three butterflies, one each to represent my two half-sisters and me. The inscription read, "It was your voice that gave us wings." (A slight twist on the Garth Brooks tune.) When all was complete, I even received a digital photo of the new headstone by email. The total cost was around $600—much less than I had imagined, especially since the cemetery is in an out-of-the-way place.

It felt wonderful to have this taken care of—and to give Mom a proper dedication.

. . .

The simple act of ritual allow mortals a sense of comfort and control over unseen forces, while clearing a pathway toward acceptance and closure.

Outside of receiving a floral arrangement from a friend and a sandwich tray sent over by a neighbor (both very much appreciated), all other extensions of sympathy over Dad's passing were directed toward and received by Dad's wife and family. So, after four years' worth of probate, believing our ordeal was about to end, Connie and I ached to experience some sort of reverent conclusion.

When Dad passed away it hadn't occurred to me to submit a separate obituary and arrange a separate viewing, funeral service, and reception for our own family and friends. I'm not even certain this would be considered proper funeral etiquette. But why not? Why couldn't two conflicting families each plan their own thing without butting heads? Having been deprived the opportunity to begin with, I wondered, why couldn't we still?

I discussed the possibility with Connie. Empowered by the idea of holding our very own memorial service for Dad, we set a date—St. Patrick's Day. Connie made her travel reservations, and we waited for the probate to end.

It didn't. While gathering papers for the final report—papers that had been dropped off and filed at my attorney's office—I discovered another asset, and then another, and another. You see, over the years, each time I found a possible estate asset, I'd hand the information to the receptionist assuming she would pass my latest find along to the attorney.

I'd brought them in to the office drip-by-drip because I always thought that "this one" would be the last I would find. When, during one of our "final" meetings, the attorney stated that my father's estate essentially consisted of his house and a couple of other items, I assumed he had looked over everything and decided nothing else belonged to the estate. Turned out he didn't even know about the things I'd dropped off. It was a complete breakdown of communication.

Although Connie kept her travel date, we were adamant about not holding Dad's service until his estate was officially settled. Thankfully, all was not lost. One day during her visit, our need for ritual and memorial took an odd twist, leading us to the local Farmer's Market, where Connie and I happened upon a Native American medicine man selling herbs.

I recognized the smudge sticks of cedar and sage, bound in red twine resting on the corner of his table, a dollar each, according to his sign. I asked if it were true the smudging ceremony clears one's environment of leftover shadows. He looked at me with an unspoken connection I have always appreciated and have never forgotten. He simply nodded yes.

Now I realize it's easy for those of us who are generations removed from spiritual, ancestral connections to grab hold of a piece of this culture and a piece of that culture, creating a hodgepodge of New Age ritualistic nonsense. This was not my intention. I'm also aware of that ingrained human yearning deep within each of us to slow down, reclaim, revere. Everyone, eventually, must find their way back to ritual and memorial, or create one of their own.

Having been denied participation in the funeral process, I found comfort in the idea of the smudging ceremony and purchased two sticks. Connie treated each of us to a pair of dream catcher earrings at another table, instructing, "You and I need to catch our dreams."

Is your family tradition lost? Will separation and struggle within the family follow you to your grave? What coping tools and ritual might you leave behind, instead?

Sidewalk Philosophy

Lavender chalk drawings adorned the pathway leading from my apartment to the parking lot. I stepped cautiously, taking care not to smear the unexpected reassurance that true childhood still exists somewhere other than cyberspace. The sidewalk masterpiece created by phantom children, was my proof.

The graffiti ended just next to the handicap ramp with a declaration "I WAS HERE" framed by preschool scribble.

A tossed aside piece of half used sidewalk chalk peeked through nearby grass, teasing me. I looked around. I didn't see anyone, but it's always hard to tell who might be watching. I didn't hear anyone, but it's 116 degrees. What would I expect to hear other than the struggling unified hum of electricity?

Dare I? Double dare??

I laughed at my thought of becoming known as the Crazy Chalk Lady. (Or Crazy Lady Who Stands on Sidewalk Laughing—at nothing.) But I had to do it. I double-dared myself. Quickly I bent, grabbed the chalk and, careful not to touch the scorching, egg-frying concrete added--

WILL IT MATTER THAT I WAS?

At exactly 10:00 p.m. that night, the automatic sprinklers turned on and washed it all away.

The difference between Skeptics and True Believers is not that Skeptics believe what is sensible and obvious, while True Believers accept what is fanciful and far-fetched. Often, it is the other way around.

CHET RAYMO, SKEPTICS AND TRUE BELIEVERS

Soul Searching

When I first began this writing project, I decided I must include some information on psychic mediums. After all, for a multitude of anguished souls, the medium represents their last, best hope at seeking reassurance of an afterlife. The medium also embodies a last crapshoot chance to set things right with the dead—a chance to communicate what wasn't said, but should have been said, way back when the dead were alive.

At the time, probably as a result of 9/11, a few well-known clairvoyants were making their talk show rounds. John Edward hosted a popular television show called *Crossing Over with John Edward* on cable's Sci-Fi Channel. I liked him. I liked his attitude and the advice he gave. He encouraged communication and validation among the living *before* it's too late, which was the very foundation of my book. So, wouldn't it be great if he granted me an interview?

My personal belief was that whether or not the psychic part was real or imagined wasn't as important as the mental comfort and closure Edward seemed to provide. That would be my angle. I would write a chapter titled: "The Need for John Edward." A couple of years later, I saw he was scheduled to come to Vegas. I bought two tickets online, and then called "his people" to request an interview. I left a voicemail.

The quick response recorded on my answering machine said, as a rule, John Edward does not give interviews to anyone other than the media, and it ended with, "Good luck on your book."

After researching his life and work, I had concluded that he would be approachable. So much for *my* psychic abilities. In retrospect, I'm thankful he wasn't, because it allowed me to experience the event without the weight of obligation. But I must say it is a tad unnerving to be denied an interview with a psychic medium. The rejection left a sense of foreboding, as in: *Does he know something I don't know about my book?*

Billed as "reading intensive," the total cost for two general admission tickets was $172.50. The event was held on a Sunday afternoon tucked away inside a brightly lit meeting room at the Sands Expo/Venetian. A security guard said they were expecting one thousand attendees, but it felt smaller. Like the end of a fad.

Sections of folding-chair seating fanned out before a small, center-front stage. Mindful of the sit-too-close-and-the-teacher-will-call-on-you threat, my daughter and I chose a secure spot in the back to the right, hopefully shielded by distance. We did not—make that DID NOT—desire a reading, real or imagined. With our luck, we joked, only "the evil one" (without naming names) would show up.

The room was warm, which surprised me. I had theorized a room conducive to active spirits would need to be cool, if not cold—a matter of quantum physics. Perhaps this is true, because one of the first things

Edward mentioned when he stepped onto the stage was about how warm it was. "Does room temperature affect a spirit's ability to come through?" I imagined asking during the not-going-to-happen interview.

Edward searched the crowd. With a wave of his hand he implied he was being drawn toward the very center of the audience and asked, "Is there a Snooky here?"

Completely blindsided by the impact of that question, my heart jumped into my throat and flopped back down inside my chest, thumping so hard I was certain I would implode. *Snooky? Oh, my God. I'm Snooky. Omigod!*

"Right here," he said, zeroing in on a woman as he described her clothing. An assistant handed her a mic. The woman stood.

"Do you have a Snooky?"

It's me, it's me, I screamed inside. *Dad called me Snooky all the time.*

"Yes," the lady said. "My cousin's name was Snooky."

How could there be two Snookys in one room? I'm certain he means me. I hadn't even thought about Dad calling me that in years. Years! And come to think of it, why did Dad call me Snooky? What the hell is a Snooky, anyhow?

The pounding in my chest would not ease. My attention to the reading faded in and out.

"There is something about baseball," Edward said. No, the woman couldn't think of anything. Edward is certain. "Yes. Something about baseball and—at the bat."

Oh, My God! This is for ME! Dad's name was Casey. I always used to say, "Casey at the bat."

No, it just didn't mean anything to the lady.

It IS Dad. Should I raise my hand? Wait! What am I thinking? I don't want a reading, and he hasn't been drawn this way at all. And the lady has been validating other things so the reading must be for her.

Edward was stumped by the number two. He kept saying there are "two." *Could the problem be that there really are two Snookys? Maybe he's getting two readings mixed together? Hers and mine.*

Before the event, Edward had instructed the crowd that it was possible for readings to commingle. He also noted that oftentimes the recipient doesn't immediately understand the information offered. Frequently, the information doesn't click at all until sometime after the reading.

"There are two Als," he stated, perplexed.

Hmm. The new manager at my daughter's workplace is named Al. I have a friend named Allison who uses Al in email. I have a niece named Allison. Growing up we had a neighbor named Al. A and L are the first initials of my husband's first name and mine. Good grief, I'm really stretching. Now just listen to the reading. Focus.

"Somebody is blind over here," Edward waved his hand, again gesturing toward the center of the crowd. There was no immediate validation, and I thought my heart would truly explode.

Oh. My. God. Mom was blind. This has to be for me!

Somebody loves to cook, he said.

Mom! Mom LOVED cooking. She was known for her cooking. She was going to write a cookbook. Two weeks before she died, she told me that if she got better, she would never clean house again. She would hire a housekeeper and write her book.

The lady claimed that validation, as well, acknowledging that it was indeed her cousin who loved to cook.

Edward and his unseen guides continued to work the room. I continued to claim a name here, a date there, a tidbit of information "no one else could have possibly known," offered to a family in the front row, way over there. The entire event had become my very own (impersonalized) scattered reading as I followed the cues in reserved silence. Until . . .

Edward's attention drifted toward our section. There was something about an interracial marriage, he said. Before I had time to blink, a middle-aged woman in the row directly behind us raised her hand.

"Yes," she acknowledged; this was for her.

"Really?" Edward asked, sounding a bit uncertain. "Who was interracial?"

The woman stood and, without hesitation, offered what I felt was a questionable tale of yore, which began, "Well, my great-great-great-grandfather married a- -"

Oh, Lordy, talk about reaching. And in a snap, I awakened from my self-imposed trance.

The experience haunted me for days. I even felt I had cheated myself by not speaking up. That *maybe* the first reading was meant for me. That perhaps I should have waved my hand in the air and jumped up spouting excitable, wasting-time ramblings, revealing more personal information than anyone really cared to listen to even though we had been instructed in the beginning not to do so.

I tried to be rational, objective. But I kept looking back. I hadn't attended in hope of making contact with anyone "over there." Yet a sense of unfinished business was determined to hang around. I just couldn't shake that feeling of *almost*.

Living in Las Vegas, one has a tendency to think in terms of almost, as in, "I almost got three sevens; or I almost hit twenty-one; or I was so close—all I needed was a five." The wise, however, quickly learn there is no almost in gambling. Gambling is an absolute. Either you win or you don't. And for sanity's sake, when you walk away from a slot machine or a table, you close your ears and never, *ever*, look back. You don't want to leave a machine for someone else to immediately take over and then watch them hit the jackpot. Talk about Vegas regret!

Then there are times when despite knowing better—just like Lot's wife—you can't help but look back.

I had walked into the event without expectation. I walked out with questions. What about the ones who attended, certain they would find answers? How many other *almosts* were in the crowd that afternoon? How many desperate souls were sent back home to wallow in uncertainty as intense as before? How many found reassurance? Are each of us connected by common threads woven from one life into another, so not one single life is truly that unique?

So many questions. But in the end, there remain things we just can't know—questions that cannot be answered. And ultimately, in this lifetime, we arrive at that point in the road divided into three choices of perspective: to believe, to not believe, or to wait and see. It is in the last of these where I find faith—and the one place out of the three where I believe mortals truly can go to find peace.

Nothing is covered up that will not be revealed, or hidden that will not be known. Whatever you have said in the dark shall be heard in the light, and what you have whispered in private rooms shall be proclaimed upon the housetops.

Luke 12:2-3

What's That Rattling?

My grandmother and I hadn't been in contact for over two years, when she suddenly passed away. After the third night of her passing, I dreamt she walked into my son's nursery, peeked inside his crib, walked into my room, kissed me on the cheek goodbye and said she had come to find out what had happened to me. Then, within that mystical realm unique to the subconscious, we shared a silent understanding as her image melded into eternity.

The dream sustained me in perfect solace for the next twenty years. It wasn't until well after Dad's passing, when I began the task of sorting through the chaos left behind, that hidden pieces of our family truths began to emerge.

Among the pieces found were my grandmother's address book and a letter she had written to my father one month before she died. Below my name in the address book were three separate entries of bogus, scratched-out addresses. Her letter read: "Please send me Ann's address again and please print it clearly and large enough this time so I can read it. I would like to be able to write to her. What is the name of the university she is attending? I hope that she is doing well. I worry about her. I have always felt that she is a lonely soul."

Dad was ashamed that I was not attending college and had encouraged me to sever all ties with my grandmother to keep her from finding out the horrible truth. Two decades later, a box of personal papers presented the revelation that he had manipulated the situation even further, thus ensuring our separation. And with great sadness I discovered that my grandmother had not easily let go.

What's in your closet?

. . .

Whose Photo Is This and Why Should I Care?— Preservation of family history and has become extremely important to the boomer generation. I felt fortunate to be able to retrieve our family photos, my grandmother's scrapbooks and miscellaneous cards and letters. But there are still so many gaps and mysteries.

- Interview family and record history before it's too late. Spending time with the elderly, ill, or any family member, to listen and allow them time to reminiscence, to validate their stories, is a calming and comforting act of love.
- No longer tangibly stored inside a box, or albums in grandma's closet, today most photos are stored on personal cell phones and/or somewhere in the clouds. Have you thought about how, or if, your children and future generations will be able to locate and preserve any meaningful family photos after you are gone?

- To learn how to trace your family history, consider joining your local Genealogical Society, or the National Genealogical Society online, which offers a comprehensive site with free resources. Or look for Genealogy classes and seminars through continuing education courses, your local library and through other community resources.
- Genealogy retrieval, storage, software and DNA test kits are available online.
- Tracing family history makes a terrific summer project for kids.
- Don't forget to identify the people and places in your photos.

Make your wishes clear
Make your wishes known
Make your wishes legal

Guessing Game

Not that long ago, a body didn't have many end-of-life issues to consider. Most bodies didn't give the matter any thought at all. Before life support, organ transplant, and sci-fi dabbling into life-extension techniques, it was almost a given that a body would die naturally and be buried naturally in a plot alongside the rest of its kinfolk. Today a body might find itself subjected to a variety of medical intrusions—before, or who knows, maybe even while—meeting its maker. Imagine being in the presence of God, only to have this exchange:

God: And the meaning of life is- -

Soul: Uh, God, excuse me just a minute, could you hold that thought? Some body is beeping in on the other line. Let me check. Yep. They're shouting something about not going toward the light. Hold on. I'll be right back—I think.

God: Oh, dear *Me*, when will they ever learn? Exactly what part of "mortal" don't they understand?

Unfortunately, our human mindset hasn't caught up with the medical reality here on the ground. We still think in terms of having nothing much to worry about regarding physical end-of-life events. Or, somewhere in the back of our minds, we understand there are things we need to consider, but not right now. Then comes along a high-profile Terri Schiavo situation, with the resulting surge of public concern.

Wow, we shudder, she was so young. What if this were to happen to us?

Regardless of age, we all need to secure our instructions in writing, because that plea you made to your sister back in 1988 while the two of you were watching a movie together does not count as an Advance Directive. Even if she does remember you begging Please, oh please, if that happens to me, don't let them put me on life support!

Should the unfortunate need arise where she would be called upon to defend your "wishes," don't pass the burden onto her alone to try and convince everyone else that life-loving you said no way to life-support way back when. (Please, oh please.)

For access to state specific forms and for more information, check out FiveWishes.org.

Spare Parts

Organ Donation, a.k.a. Anatomical Gifts, is one tough subject. But chances are one day each of us will either be faced with making a donor decision on behalf of a loved one or unwittingly become an organ donor, ourselves. Here again, medical technology is bulldozing its way into our lives as never before.

How many unprepared families have been thrown into the murky territory of being told a loved one is "gone" in the same moment they are asked to donate the loved one's organs? At a moment when they simply need to breathe. To cry. To process. They must make a rational decision on something so emotionally intrusive as body parts.

Literature in favor of organ harvesting remind us of a "critical organ shortage," that a donation is a "gift of life," and that twenty-two people (2018) die each day while waiting for a match. Talk about being placed on the spot. To deny a donation and thereby deny a fellow being hope—or life—is a mighty heavy chain to drag around.

Some families eagerly grasp the concept their loved one would live on through the life of another—that an action of donation would give meaning to their loss. Other families aren't prepared to take on such a view. Both, however, are worthy of honor and respect because no one in this world can know with certainty which outlook is correct. No one should have to endure tactics of being bullied, coerced, belittled, or showered with guilt into agreeing. This is a personal, sacred choice.

. . .

Cellular Memory: A hypothesis claiming an individual's memories, tastes, and habits—everything that makes us who we are—are recorded and stored inside our cells. In the case of organ donation, some believe such individualized recorded memories are passed on from the donor to the recipient on a cellular level through an organ (especially the heart), and the organ recipient may be aware of, or take on, the transplanted traits.

∙ ∙ ∙

About Face—In November 2004, the Cleveland Clinic became the first U.S. medical facility approved to perform the world's first full-face transplant. However, Spain was the first to perform the procedure in 2010.

A transplant from a brain-dead organ donor might include the face, both ears, a full head of hair, and other features, together in one piece. Unlike the movie Face Off, a recipient would not take on the donors' features, but instead become a hybrid of their former self and donor.

France and China, respectively, became the first countries to perform partial-face transplants.

We rarely think of it as such, but skin is the body's largest organ.

∙ ∙ ∙

Getting into Harvard—Despite urban myth, you can't sell your body or organs to a medical school. (Search Snopes.com, organ transplants) However, you might donate your body to Harvard Medical School through the Anatomical Gifts Program. The Harvard Brain Tissue Resource Center accepts brain donations. Or contact a medical school or willed body program of your choice.

Note: Unlike organ donation, body donation is unregulated. Often, you'll have no idea exactly where your donated body will end up or how it will be used, despite having specified your wishes in writing.

• • •

One last chance—In the news: A twenty-eight-year-old widow of a soldier killed in Iraq petitioned for and was granted a federal court order allowing for the extraction and preservation of her husband's sperm, for artificial insemination in hope of conceiving the couple's first child.

The order blocked the soldier's mother, who disapproved of the procedure, from arranging for the embalmment and disposal of her son's remains until a medical representative could extract the sperm.

• • •

Dude, **where's my kidney?**—Have you heard the urban legend about the college student party dude (or traveling salesman or tourist) who wakes up naked in a bathtub filled with ice and missing a kidney?

According to 2008 news articles and televised reports, for nearly a decade, such myth may have been reality in India, where Indian police busted a horrific illegal transplant ring. At the time, investigators believed this ring was involved with as many as five hundred illegal transplants of kidneys and other organs stolen from the poor and unemployed who were lured by the promise of a job, and then drugged and their organs removed.

• • •

Out-sourced—Transplant business boomed as people throughout the world, unable to receive a transplant elsewhere, scored matches in China. According to a CNN/Anderson Cooper 360° report titled, "Prisoners' Organs," which aired in December 2006:

China-based transplant services, known as "Organ Tourism," advertised through websites, offered heart, lung, and other organ transplants for up to $200,000.

After arriving in China, a potential organ recipient and his wife were provided a cell phone by the hospital where the transplant was to take place. They were instructed to enjoy the sights until the phone rang, signaling a match had been found. The match for a new liver took only two weeks.

Some American doctors—aware of the potential violation of human rights—have refused to treat patients who receive transplants in China.

Over the years, testimony presented before Congress by Human Rights Activists accused the Chinese government of harvesting organs from death-row prisoners without their consent.

In the United States, death-row inmates are not allowed to donate their organs.

Living Donor: My Choice

SHELLEY MARQUEZ

I was a junior in college when I first heard about bone marrow transplants. The campus newspaper ran a story about a Hispanic student who needed a transplant and how the search to find a compatible donor had been unsuccessful. Hispanic students were urged to sign up for blood tests to see if a match were among them.

Upon reading the story, I felt an overwhelming desire to help. When I told friends and family about my decision, I received mixed responses. Many didn't understand why I would help. But my mind was made up. Even though there was a slim chance I would match this student, at least I tried.

I wasn't a match after all, but I had become an official bone marrow donor, and it felt right. My reasoning: I am not an organ donor. I never would be. But as a bone marrow donor I am still helping and, if I am a match, I will be alive to experience the whole process.

Five years after being on the donor list, I finally received the call. I was told I was a potential match and asked if I still wanted to participate. "Of course," I replied, "this is why I signed up!"

After playing a game of one hundred questions with the organization and allowing seven tubes to be filled with my blood, it was confirmed. I was a definite match. Unfortunately, for reasons not revealed, the patient no longer needed me. But since more of my blood is now on file, my chance of being matched with others in the future has increased.

• • •

National Marrow Donor Program (NMDP):

To locate a center near you or to learn more about the process, go to marrow.org or call 1-800-marrow-2.

Bredo Morstøl was a man who lived and died,
at age eighty-nine, in Norway.
His remains lie inside a steel coffin
chained and welded shut,
tightly packed in dry ice,
placed inside an insulated wooden box
upon a concrete slab
stored inside a Tuff Shed
sitting on a mountainside
overlooking the Continental Divide
in Nederland, Colorado, USA.

A Winter Festival

Once an unassuming Norwegian, Bredo is known worldwide in death as Grandpa in the Tuff Shed: centerpiece for the annual winter festival appropriately named Frozen Dead Guy Days.

On March 12, 2005, Leo, and I traveled to the tiny town of Nederland, nestled three thousand feet and a thirty-minute drive above Boulder, Colorado, to confirm that the strange winter festival I'd heard tell of the year before, really exists. That year, the festival attracted more than 7,000 enthusiastic, life-loving souls from places near and countries far.

Upon our arrival, we made our way through the noonday crowd attending the Cryogenic Parade on First Street, which consisted of various frozen and death-themed entries. After the parade, we strolled the designated path toward Chipeta Park to watch the daring participants in the Costume Polar Plunge—into the frozen lake. Next we hung out for a bit at the Tuff Shed Coffin Races, and then took a short walk up the street to B&F Market, where I made a reservation and purchased a ticket for the ninety-minute Tour of Grandpa's Tuff Shed.

Thirty minutes of free time before the next scheduled tour allowed us a quick look at the FDGD Expo and Psychic Fair across the parking lot. The Wisdom Wagon, a glass-enclosed novelty carriage occupied by a psychic and her spellbound client, sat parked outside the fair's entrance. Inside the fair were souvenir merchants; another psychic or two; and an enthusiastic cryonics advocate who stood behind a table covered with cryonics-related information.

I accepted her business card and gathered a few brochures, my favorite of which was from The Immortality Institute, a 501-3-c non-profit educational organization on a mission "to conquer the blight of involuntary death." Another favorite was the invaluable cryonics brochure of a Certified Financial Planner, because unlike heaven, (or hell) this eternity isn't free.

At the back of the room, a viewing of the documentary *Grandpa's Still in the Tuff Shed* was in progress. I purchased a copy on DVD, autographed by its delightful producers, sisters Robin and Shelly Beeck.

The tour caravan of SUVs snaked along the twisted road, yet it seemed only moments later we had arrived at the house that Grandpa's grandson, Trygve, built—an indestructible monolithic fortress of steel and raw concrete planted on the mountainside. And there, behind it, sat—*The Shed*.

Grandpa's caretaker, Bo Shaffer, a.k.a. The Iceman, of Delta Technogroup, Inc., greeted us and promptly began our tour. A personable and articulate guide, Bo is responsible for making the once-a-month drive into Nederland from Boulder to replenish 1,600 pounds of dry ice serving as life support.

When Bredo's daughter, Aud, and her son, Trygve, purchased the property, they envisioned creating the Colorado Life Extension Center. The concrete monstrosity was to be the Center's cryonics laboratory and hospice, eventually connecting with a multi-unit underground vault. But creating was slow and funds were low, and instead, the structure offered basic shelter for mother and son while Grandpa chilled out back in the makeshift vault of a garden shed.

Grandpa's unusual trek to Colorado began shortly after his death in Norway in 1989. There his body was packed in dry ice by an undertaker, and then shipped to Trans Time (a cryonics facility) in Oakland, California, where he was preserved by liquid nitrogen. In 1993, Trygve moved Gramps back onto dry ice and into a tin shed. But only a few people had known about this mountain-side scheme, and the Morstøl Family Reunion quickly rolled into one giant Colorado snowball.

Trygve was soon deported back to Norway on an expired visa, forcing him to abandon Aud, Grandpa, and the Center's first paid-customer-dead-guy, shed-mate Al Campbell, from Chicago. Next it was discovered that Aud was living in the "house" without plumbing or electricity. She was evicted. *Then* it was discovered that Aud's visa also had expired. And so, concerned about her imminent deportation, she worried out loud to a reporter that she didn't know how she would keep the bodies in the shed from thawing.

Immediately, the law was called and the frozen bodies—uncovered.

An intensive investigation found the situation strange, but legit. Al's body was returned to his family in Chicago for burial. Aud headed back to Norway before she was deported. Grandpa was allowed to remain, despite community outrage that viewed his body as a health threat. It seems that at the time there was no local ordinance against keeping a dead and/or frozen body on one's own property.

There is now.

A new ordinance forbids the storage of any frozen carcass—including a turkey in the freezer.

Time slowly thawed public opinion into acceptance and even support. When the original tin shed was ripped apart by a storm in 1995, it was replaced by a donated Tuff Shed assembled by volunteers gathered through the effort of a Denver FOX Radio promo. In 2002, the Nederland Area Chamber of Commerce conceived the idea of a winter festival.

Trygve and Aud plan to join Grandpa someday in cryonic suspension and eventual resurrection. Neither believes in the existence of the soul. And in case you've wondered, before he passed away nobody ever got around to asking Grandpa whether or not he would like to be frozen, since "he died unexpectedly."

Gathering quietly nearby, our group was joined by Aud and what appeared to be some sort of film crew. (Aud had been allowed back into the U.S. on a temporary visa to attend the festival.) Bo removed the lid of the wooden box to reveal its icy contents, and with a scurry of flashing cameras we all nudged in for a closer gawk at the horror-upon-horror sight of—boxes of dry ice. Curiosity satisfied (did we feel a tad foolish?), our cluster eased apart, allowing Aud and her crew their alone time with Gramps.

Aud stepped cautiously into the shed and turned to face the cameraman. He motioned for her to stand higher, up on the edge of the concrete platform. Then, in one brief surprisingly graceful movement, she turned, placed her hand upon the box as though it was a wounded living being, and with an amazing expression of child-like wonder, peered adoringly inside.

A giant of a man observing from a distance shook his head at me in passing, and with a heavy accent, declared, "This is strange."

I smiled in agreement but suddenly felt like a traitor in doing so. Something about that glimpse of devotion on Aud's face had just skewed my perspective.

When I first heard about a festival centered on a real dead man in a shed, the concept felt so irreverent, I was certain I could not attend. But once everything is rationalized, it becomes clear that Grandpa's situation isn't much different from his having been put to rest in a family mausoleum. Except this tomb is a Tuff Shed. And the body—on ice. Regardless of all the talk about cryonics, Grandpa is dead. Gone. Kaput. And all the reasoning, effort, and expense for keeping him frozen, simply a whole lot of to-do about nothing.

But in the words of Iceman Bo, "It's not about Death, it's about Life. Eternal Life."

As for the festival? I'd say it's a chance for a little dark-humored good time. In the earthly end, why not?

Rescuing Ted: A Lesson on Best-laid Plans

The saga of the Ted Williams's estate is a perfect example of best-laid plans and the unforeseen. Any logical, thinking person would conclude that the directive on page one, line one of Ted's will, regarding the final disposition of his body, was as clear and valid as instructions can get. Who could have known that a scrap of paper would turn up to override those specific instructions?

Who could have guessed that Mr. Williams's fate would be to spend [eternity] sealed inside a cryonics facility in Arizona?

Friday, July 5, 2002: Baseball's famed Ted Williams, age eighty-three, is pronounced dead of cardiac arrest in a hospital near his Florida home.

Saturday, July 6: Bobby-Jo Ferrell, Williams's eldest daughter by his first wife, learns that her father's remains had been transported the day before aboard a private jet to Scottsdale, Arizona, by officials from the Alcor Life Extension Foundation. These arrangements were made by John Henry Williams, Williams's son from his third marriage.

Bobby-Jo goes public with the information, accusing her half-brother, John Henry, of wanting to preserve their father's DNA in order to perhaps sell it one day.

She vows to "rescue" her father's body.

Tuesday, July 16: The Last Will and Testament of Theodore S. Williams, dated December 20, 1996, is filed and made public. In clear and precise language under Article 1–1 Cremation/Funeral, Ted Williams requests:

Cremation. I direct that my remains be cremated and my ashes sprinkled at sea off the coast of Florida where the water is very deep.

Thursday, July 25: John Henry and Claudia Williams (Williams's youngest daughter) submit an oil-stained piece of scrap paper, which they claim bears their father's signature, signed in agreement to a cryonic family pact: "JHW, Claudia, and Dad all agree to be put into biostasis after we die. This is what we want, to be able to be together in the future, even if it is only a chance."

The handwritten agreement, dated November 2, 2000, is signed by each member of the trio.

Attorney Bob Goldman states the children did not produce the agreement earlier because of "privacy issues."

When asked about the legality of the non-notarized note, Goldman informs the press that under Florida common law, persons may change their minds about the disposition of their remains without officially amending their wills.

(Changes made regarding the disposition of one's assets, however, require a notary's signature.)

Friday, December 20: Just fifteen weeks into probate and more than $87, 000 into legal-fee debt, Bobby-Jo drops all objections to the current disposition of her father's body. Through a statement read over the telephone by her husband, Mark Ferrell, she emphasizes the cost of an ongoing battle (an estimated $250,000) would be extraordinary and would "result in significant difficulties" for her family.

Bobby-Jo Ferrell is said to be at peace with her decision.

Her husband adds, "We were whipped."

March 6, 2004: John Henry Williams, age thirty-five, dies of leukemia at UCLA Medical Center. A few months earlier, he had received a bone marrow transplant from Claudia.

A family attorney declines comment as to John Henry's final wishes regarding cryonic suspension.

Update: In 2004, Williams's nephews, Sam and Ted Williams, revived the court battle to free Ted. On November 30, 2004, presiding Superior Court Judge Thomas Dunevant III of Maricopa County issued an order instructing Alcor to release the "document of gift" purportedly used to authorize the cryopreservation of Williams. Alcor initially argued against the order, but soon agreed to comply.

Nephews Sam and Ted dropped their suit in January 2005.

• • •

What the Heck Is Cryonics, Anyhow?

I don't believe in the afterlife although I am bringing a change of underwear.

Woody Allen

Father of Cryonics, Robert Ettinger, grew up with faith there would someday be a cure for disease and old age. When he realized this probably wasn't going to be a day during his lifetime, he decided he'd better start doing something to encourage things along. So, in 1948, Ettinger wrote a short story that was published in a science fiction magazine—his first attempt to direct public interest toward his cause.

Not too many people noticed.

In 1962, a second attempt to reel in a following snagged on a failed letter-writing campaign after having contacted a few hundred select names from "Who's Who in America." Ettinger then realized that a successful rally of support would require a book-length explanation of his vision of a cure for death. That same year he created, and privately published, a preliminary version of *The Prospect of Immortality*.

People noticed.

In 1964, Doubleday published the first commercial version of the book.

More people noticed.

And so the cryonics movement began.

The result of Ettinger's effort is the speculative practice of whole-body (or head/brain tissue) preservation through a process called *vitrification*, more commonly referred to as "freezing."

Ideally, the process begins when life support is used to restore blood circulation and brain viability within minutes after the patient is declared legally dead. The goal of cryonics is to intercept the dying process and to preserve "life" in a viable state until future medical advances such as nanotechnology or cloning might reanimate the body.

The history of cryonics is filled with so many bizarre and, at times, comical tales of fact and myth that I could spend a great deal of time on the subject. Although the cryonics movement is hardly sizable, I chose to mention it simply because it exists and because the possibility exists for anyone to end up frozen in time—by no conscious choice of their own. All it takes for having one's remains diverted from traditional burial to a cryonic storage facility (or shed) is an unforeseen decision made by a durable health care agent or the misdirected use of an anatomical gift document.

Today, as never before, we must take time to educate ourselves regarding what the future might hold, and of what precautions we might need to take to protect ourselves from that great unknown.

Art Buchwald, "The Man Who Wouldn't Die"

In January 2006, at age eighty, world-famous political satire columnist Art Buchwald decided enough was enough. He chose not to spend the rest of his life—five hours a day, three days a week—hooked up to and dependent upon a dialysis machine.

So, dialysis treatments were stopped, and end-of-life arrangements were made. He would check into a Washington, DC, hospice and go about the business of leaving this world naturally.

His doctor gave him two to three weeks. Instead, Buchwald thrived, "having the time of my life." He dined on whatever he wanted—including McDonald's hamburgers and milkshakes. He thrived socially with fellow patients and friends who came pouring in from everywhere to say goodbye. He granted interviews, received awards, and planned his memorial service. Months later, he had thrived so well, he was sent back to his home on Martha's Vineyard, where he began writing his column again and composed an entire book about his life experience with death. It seemed he would live on forever. But sadly—or rather, gently—his time did arrive.

On January 17, 2007, at age eighty-one, Art Buchwald passed away, peaceful, happy and loved.

> **Right to Die:** *The first Death with Dignity Act was enacted on October 27, 1997, in the state of Oregon, allowing "terminally-ill Oregonians to end their lives through the voluntary self-administration of lethal medications, expressly prescribed by a physician for that purpose."*
>
> *As of 2019, physician-assisted suicide is a legal option in seven states, plus the District of Columbia.*

My guide and I came on that hidden road to make our way back into the bright world; and with no care for any rest, we climbed— he first, I following—until I saw, through a round opening, some of those things of beauty Heaven bears. It was from there that we emerged, to see— once more—the stars.

Dante Alighieri, The Divine Comedy: Inferno; Purgatorio; Paradiso, *(translation by Allen Mandelbaum)*

In the Ending That Finally Was Found

> *The jury all wrote down, on their slates,*
>
> *"SHE doesn't believe there's an atom of meaning in it."*
>
> *"If there's no meaning in it," said the King,*
>
> *"that saves a world of trouble, you know,*
>
> *as we needn't try to find any."*
>
> LEWIS CARROLL, ALICE'S ADVENTURES IN WONDERLAND

Throughout every form of inheritance planning, we are warned to avoid the costly, time-consuming devil called probate. But other than the image of this money-hungry monster insatiably feasting upon courses of one's inheritance over the span of several years, what do people really know about the process?

Before my appointment as personal representative, I attempted to demystify this great unknown by reading everything on the subject I could find. I read the New Mexico Probate Code, skimmed through volumes upon volumes of library books for reference and guidance, and of course, retained legal counsel. I understood the sole purpose of probate was for the judge to give authorization of the transfer of estate assets. Yet, up until the very end, I fantasized that a Perry Mason courtroom moment of cornered, spontaneous confession would save us. And right up to that very last day as we sat before the judge seeking approval for finalization of estate, I held this faith, this erroneous belief, that at some point the law would intercede and set things right. But this is not its purpose.

With an uneventful nod from the judge and the official stamping of documents by a court clerk—after five long years—it was over. I stood faith-shattered, left with the feeling that nothing had even been questioned or scrutinized. There would be no diligent seeking of truths, no wrongs set right. All of the years spent, the tears shed, my seeking of truth now seemed so irrelevant. In a moment tangled in relief and frustration, there was nothing left to say or do. It was over.

The end of a time of intentions gone bad. All rise!

• • •

Taxes, probate, privacy—these are the trigger words hammered into our minds by the living trust movement, and the words used to incite rebellion against traditional wills and mistrust toward the attorneys who create them.

One might easily assume that, as a victim and survivor of a probate lasting over five years, I would blame probate for all of my estate-settling sorrows. However, as I have emphasized throughout this book, probate was not the problem. In the scheme of things, it had very little impact upon Dad's estate at all.

A probate court order *did* provide me the opportunity to go onto Dad's property and take possession. But it did not help define Dad's intentions, locate assets, investigate or retrieve missing assets. Likewise, it was not responsible for dragging out the process, for attorney fees or for high estate-settling costs.

Probate did not create years of toil and trouble—the people involved did.

. . .

So, what about all of those privacy concerns? To find out for myself, I journeyed back to my hometown on a sultry, overcast day in late summer 2003 to the place where this life chapter ends—back to the courthouse and its notorious public records of probate.

After passing through the metal detector arch set up just inside the doorway, I asked the security guard if he could direct me to the office where the probate files are viewed. He had no idea and sent me to the information desk where the receptionist gave me the impression my question had never been asked before. At last, she directed me down the hall and to the right, to the same office where the clerk had stamped the final court documents on the day Dad's probate was closed.

Inside, a woman ahead of me at the window asked for a form and quickly left. I gave the clerk Dad's name and case number and requested his file. Without asking *my* name or why I needed to view the information, she picked up a phone and placed the order.

"This will take a couple of minutes," she said. "Have a seat at the next window, and I will bring it to you."

As promised, it didn't take long for her to deliver the thick file. She said to take my time and even offered to make copies if needed. It felt strange to hold everything again. In a way, being there even felt wrong, like I was snooping. Yet, the contents were all too familiar—every single sheet, from beginning to end.

Skimming through the pages representing five years' worth of grief took me less than five minutes. One minute per year.

I returned the documents to the clerk, who again offered to make copies. Glancing at the sign on the counter that warned "We reserve the right to deny requests for copies," I couldn't help but smile at her eagerness. I thanked her and explained that I was conducting research for a book and that I was curious about how often people actually come in and request to view a file.

She said, "Rarely, and anyone who does is usually a family member during the time that probate is open."

"How long are the records kept in storage?"

Her answer, "Indefinitely."

When I arrived, I had considered requesting Stepmum's information, as well, but decided against it. The thought of rummaging through the details of her estate *really* felt like snooping and—in the end—would serve no purpose other than to conjure up bad feelings. Instead, having retraced my steps to the beginning and to the end, I turned and walked outside into an unexpected gift of radiant sunshine and peace.

"Begin at the beginning,"
the King said gravely,
"and go on till you come to the end:
then stop."
    Lewis Carroll, Alice's Adventures in Wonderland

In the last dream about my father,
he's sitting in a chair
a great distance away from me,
engulfed in darkness
as though suspended in deep space.
He speaks one word: Velocity.
And then, he's gone.

ABOUT THE AUTHOR

Ann Marquez is a compulsive fact checker, seeker of truth, political junkie, writer, and artist. Currently living in the American Southwest with her husband, and a hand-me-down cat named Ruby, she is surrounded by an entourage of muses offering too much inspiration for one lifetime.

www.ingramcontent.com/pod-product-compliance
Lightning Source LLC
Chambersburg PA
CBHW051946290426
44110CB00015B/2124